The New
Chinese Cooking
for Health and Fitness

© 1986 Lydia Wang

Published by GAKKEN CO., LTD.
4-40-5 Kami-ikedai, Ohta-ku, Tokyo, Japan

Overseas Distributor: Japan Publications Trading Co., Ltd.
P.O.Box 5030 Tokyo International, Tokyo, Japan

Distributors:
United States: Kodansha International/USA, Ltd., through Harper & Row, Publishers, Inc., 10 East 53rd Street, New York, N.Y. 10022
South America: Harper & Row, Publishers, Inc., International Department
Canada: Fitzhenry & Whiteside Ltd., 195 Allstate Parkway, Markham, Ontario L3R 4T8
British Isles: International Book Distributors Ltd., 66 Wood Lane End, Hemel Hempstead, Herts HP2 4RG
Australia and New Zealand: Bookwise International, 1 Jeanes Street, Beverley, South Australia 5007
The Far East and Japan: Japan Publications Trading Co., Ltd., 1-2-1, Sarugaku-cho, Chiyoda-ku, Tokyo 101

First Printing 1986

ISBN: 0-87040-730-9
ISBN: 4-05-150596-0 (in Japan)
Printed in Japan

Credits:
The following companies generously contributed cooking and serving utensils for use in photographs appearing in this book.
Kosta Boda Japan Branch
Paris Scandals
Richard Ginori
Rosenthal
Suita Trading Corporation
Toshiba Corporation
Wedgwood Japan

Book design
Kazumi Aoyama
Photography
Aritoshi Nakasato
Tableware coordinator
Izumi Ishimori
Nutritional data
Fukiko Takeuchi
(Calonic Diet Studio)

Lydia Wang

The New Chinese Cooking

for Health and Fitness

Preface

There is an old Chinese saying that states "Medicine and food are of a kind." This is a rather terse way of saying that our daily dietary habits form the basis for the prevention and cure of illness, so that food, like medicine, is important.

That concept even now is very much alive in Chinese cooking, where much consideration is given to what ingredients should make up each dish, how those ingredients should be cooked and with what others combined in order to maintain and promote health. This book, needless to say, fully subscribes to that concept. There is, however, a point on which traditional Chinese cooking is at variance with contemporary views on health.

Chinese cooking has always used a lot of oil—so much in fact that it is a characteristic of Chinese cooking in general. Oil, however, is a food high in calories so that when you count them in oil-rich Chinese cooking the number is invariably high, even if it were possible to deduct those that remain in the oil in the pan after cooking or on the plate after eating.

On the other hand, a major health problem nowadays is the increase every year in the number of people who are overweight, primarily because of overeating and a lack of exercise. Or, put another way, because the number of calories taken in by the body exceeds the number expended.

Advances made by civilization over the years have certainly contributed much to making life easier and more convenient; yet it is also true that not all such advances have necessarily been beneficial to our health. The development of the car as a method of transportation, for example, has also helped to bring about a lowering in the physical activity level of people. Thus, in many cases a low expenditure of calories stemming from a lack of exercise results in being overweight even though a person may be convinced he or she is not overeating.

Being overweight is bad because it makes a person susceptible to such health problems as diabetes, heart disease, liver trouble, high blood pressure and so on. Health is a life-long treasure that cannot be bought with money, and obstacles to it should not be given a chance to start.

The phrase "Health and Fitness" in the title of this book is aimed at helping to prevent or overcome the problem of being overweight. To accomplish that, the intake of calories must be controlled and a nutritional balance maintained. Undeniably, traditional Chinese cooking is high in calories and in need of new innovations. It has now been some 30 years since I first started giving lessons in home-style Chinese cooking in Japan, and during that time I have keenly felt the need to do something to bring it more into line with contemporary ideas on health. This book is one result of that conviction and, in that sense, is quite different from books on traditional Chinese cooking.

In the writing of this book I have tried to adhere to five basic points. The first was to produce a book that would, wherever possible, introduce new and low-calorie Chinese dishes. An example of this is the pre-dinner salad appearing in the section on Appetizers. It is a healthful dish not found in traditional Chinese cooking and is a result of my own research and studies.

The second guiding point was to try to be freely creative with traditional Chinese cooking, reducing oil to the absolute minimum, varying the ingredients, re-working the preliminary cooking preparations and experimenting with all manner of new ideas so as to lower the caloric intake. The result has been a reduction in calories by at least 20–30 percent.

Thirdly, I avoided wherever possible any special or peculiar ingredients, opting instead for those that are readily available.

My fourth guideline was that I should introduce dishes that can easily be made by anyone without any special equipment or great mastery in cooking, for I believe that no matter how good a dish might be for health and fitness, if it cannot be made easily then there is not much point in including it. Not a few cookbooks that have come under my inspection show dishes that are attractive and tempting but formidable to make.

The fifth point that I followed was to try to present food that is good to eat. Though designed for health and fitness, the dishes in this book have by no means been adapted at the expense of their original good taste. They are good to eat. Food, after all, is not just something to fill an empty stomach or maintain and promote good health. It is also a means of making life better. Good food enriches the quality of our everyday meals, and a rich and varied table can be the foundation of happiness in the home.

It has been my hope that by writing this book people throughout the world will, through these Chinese dishes of mine, enjoy health and happiness.

Lydia Wang

Tokyo, March 30, 1986

Contents

How To Use This Book

The Chinese dishes contained in this book are easily made at home, good to eat and good for you as an aid to health and fitness. I have adapted the original Chinese dishes so as to lower the caloric and fat content, and have included numerous others of my own design that are quite unlike the Chinese dishes of the past.

Calorie Count and Nutritional Information

As an aid to dieters, I have indicated the calorie count for each dish along with the amounts of carbohydrates (excluding dietary fiber), proteins, and fats and oils. The figures—or even when there are none—are all for servings per person. *The Japanese Food Composition Table* served as the basis for all of the calculations.

Format of the Recipes

For each recipe there is a color photograph of the finished dish and, appearing with it, detailed instructions for preparation and cooking. For particularly complex preparations, small photographs have been added to demonstrate technique.

Weights and Measures

The weights and measures used in the list of ingredients and cooking instructions for each recipe are given in both the metric and standard American-British system of pounds and ounces. British cooks measure many more items by weight than do Americans, who prefer cup measurements for items such as rice, flour, chopped vegetables, and so on. When following the recipes, use the measurement you are most comfortable with.

Liquid measurements present more of a problem when a book is to be used by cooks in different countries. The Japanese cup, for example, measures 200 ml, whereas the American cup is 236 ml, the British cup is 284 ml, and the Australian cup is 250 ml. Since most of the ingredients measured in these recipes are of small quantities, these differences should not be a problem for cooks in any country. However, in dealing with quantities over 4 cups, we suggest you use the following conversion chart:

Liquid Measures—Conversion Chart (Cup Measures)

American Cup (in book)	United Kingdom Adjusts to:	Australia Adjusts to:
4 cups (2 pints)	1½ pints + 3 tablespoons	1½ pints − 3 tablespoons

A Note on Tools and Ingredients

Most Chinese dishes can be made in a wok. Where no mention of any particular utensil is made in the recipes of this book, you can take it to mean that a wok should be used. For information on its use, please refer to page 107. If a wok is not available, a large frying pan will suffice.

In this book, vegetable oil is used instead of the lard ordinarily used in Chinese cooking. For rice wine, you can use either Chinese or Japanese rice wine. If they are not available, dry sherry will do. In the recipes which require vinegar, use rice vinegar for a better result.

Great care has been taken in each recipe to ensure that the ingredients used are ones readily available. To familiarize yourself with the chief ingredients in Chinese cooking, it is suggested that you consult page 116–118 where they are listed.

APPETIZERS

Appetizers are just about a must when pre-dinner drinks are to be served. They should be something that can easily be made at home and, preferably, well ahead of time. Although one plate featuring appetizers all of one kind will often suffice, a more elaborate presentation would be to have a plate of mixed types. Fancier yet would be several plates featuring a variety on each, and for a really grand show you might consider a plate with appetizers set out in the form of a Chinese phoenix, a dragon or some other such symbol of good luck and fortune. The appetizers selected for this section have purposely been chosen and adapted for a low fat-content and small volume of oil.

Cold Poached Shrimp
Chicken with Spicy Sauce
Shrimp Toast

Deep-Fried Mushrooms
Soy Sauce Beef

Cold Poached Shrimp

4 servings
Cooking time:
10 minutes
½ pound (250g) shrimp
1 tablespoon finely julienned
   fresh ginger
1 tablespoon rice wine
1 star anise
2 teaspoons salt
1½ cups water
Garnish: Parsley

A simple recipe calling for small, fresh shrimp to be quickly boiled in the shell. Best when served cold.

Calories 31	Protein 5.4g	Fats 0.3g	Carbohydrates 0.6g

1. Devein shrimp and remove only legs.
2. Save half of ginger for garnish by placing it in cold water until ready to use.
3. Combine the remaining half of ginger, rice wine, star anise, and salt with the water. Bring to a boil and cook shrimp 2 to 3 minutes. When color of shrimp changes, drain it well and cool.
4. Arrange shrimp on a plate. Drain ginger well and sprinkle it over shrimp. Garnish with parsley.

Chicken with Spicy Sauce

4 servings
Cooking time:
40 minutes
½ small stewing chicken
2-inch (5cm) piece of spring
   onion
2 to 3 thin slices of fresh
   ginger
1 tablespoon rice wine
Spicy sauce:
   2 tablespoons coarsely
      chopped spring onion
   1 tablespoon coarsely
      chopped fresh ginger
   1 teaspoon coarsely crushed
      whole black pepper corn
   1½ tablespoons sesame oil
   2 tablespoons soy sauce
   ½ tablespoon sugar
   ½ teaspoon salt
Garnish:
   Cilantro
   Spring onion, julienned

Boil the boned chicken until tender, then cool in the broth to retain the flavor.

Calories 323	Protein 24.6g	Fats 21.7g	Carbohydrates 3.3g

1. Place chicken in a deep pot and cover with water. Add spring onion, ginger, and rice wine. Bring to a rapid boil, skim off foam, lower heat and simmer about 40 minutes (photo). Allow chicken to cool in the broth.
2. To make spicy sauce, heat sesame oil in a small saucepan and stir-fry spring onion, ginger, and pepper. Add soy sauce, sugar, and salt. Bring to a boil, and then turn off heat.

3. Using a heavy cleaver to cut through bone, cut chicken into bite-size pieces and arrange on a plate. Garnish with cilantro, using only the leaves, and julienned spring onion. Add spicy sauce just before serving.
Note: Chicken broth can be saved for later use. You may also make a nutritious soup by adding some water, vegetables and a little salt.

To ensure a clear broth, take care to skim off as much foam as possible, as this will improve the look of chicken.

Shrimp Toast

Oil temperature is the most important factor here. Too high and the toast will burn; too low makes it soggy.

Calories 212	Protein 7.7g	Fats 16.0g	Carbohydrates 8.1g

4 servings
Cooking time:
30 minutes

1. Shell and devein shrimp. Purée them in a food processor or blender. Add seasoning to shrimp and mix well.
2. Remove crusts from bread. Spread shrimp mixture on bread slices and sprinkle with white sesame seeds.
3. Heat oil to 340°F (170°C) and gently drop bread in with shrimp side down. Deep-fry until shrimp is cooked and toast turns golden brown. Drain well and cut into bite-size pieces.
4. Arrange on a plate and garnish with lettuce leaves.

Garnish:
Lettuce leaves

½ pound (250g) shrimp
Seasoning for shrimp:
  1 teaspoon rice wine
  Dash of fresh ginger juice
  ½ teaspoon salt, 1 egg white
  1 tablespoon cornstarch
3 slices of white bread, ¼-inch (0.5cm) thick
1 tablespoon white sesame seeds
3 to 4 cups oil for deep-frying

Deep-Fried Mushrooms

Dried mushrooms will do for this low-calorie delicacy, which is an excellent substitute for meat for the orthodox Buddhist.

Calories 101	Protein 4.1g	Fats 7.5g	Carbohydrates 12.8g

4 servings
Cooking time:
40 minutes

1. Soak dried mushrooms in warm water until soft. Squeeze out any excess water, and remove stems.
2. Place mushrooms in a bowl, sprinkle ingredients for seasoning over them, and mix well.
3. Place the bowl in a steamer and steam 15 minutes.
4. Combine egg with salt, sesame oil, and vegetable oil in a bowl and mix well. Add cornstarch and mix well.
5. Heat oil to 360°F (180°C). Meanwhile, pat mushrooms dry before coating them with batter and deep-fry them until golden.
6. Arrange mushrooms on a plate and garnish with parsley.

Garnish:
Parsley

16 dried mushrooms
Seasoning for mushrooms:
  2 teaspoons rice wine
  1 teaspoon salt
  1 teaspoon sugar
  Dash of fresh ginger juice
  2 tablespoons chicken broth
Batter: 1 egg, pinch of salt
  ½ teaspoon sesame oil
  ½ tablespoon vegetable oil
  3½ tablespoons cornstarch
3 to 4 cups oil for deep-frying

Soy Sauce Beef

Calories 185	Protein 30.1g	Fats 3.3g	Carbohydrates 5.5g

8 servings
Cooking time:
1 hour
40 minutes

1. Blanch beef until color changes. Remove and rinse well under running water.
2. In a deep pot, place beef, spring onion, ginger, rice wine, soy sauce, sugar, and water to cover. Bring to a boil, and then simmer about 1½ hours or until beef is tender. Allow beef to cool in the broth.
3. Slice beef and arrange the slices on a plate with spring onion and ginger.

Garnish: Spring onion and fresh ginger, julienned

2 pounds (1kg) boneless beef shank
4-inch (10cm) piece of spring onion
1 teaspoon julienned fresh ginger
¼ cup rice wine
2 cups soy sauce
2 tablespoons sugar

Radish and Cucumber Salad
Vermicelli Salad
Salmon and Beancurd Salad

Crabmeat and Chicken Salad

Assorted Vegetable Salad

Radish and Cucumber Salad

4 servings
Preparation time:
5 minutes
8 radishes
4 ounces (100g) cucumber
Dressing:
  1 tablespoon soy sauce
  ½ tablespoon vinegar
  2 teaspoons sesame oil
  ¼ teaspoon sugar

Even the most inept can make this healthful appetizer.

Calories 27	Protein 0.7g	Fats 2.1g	Carbohydrates 1.3g

1. Cut tops off radishes. Using the broad side of a cleaver or a rolling pin, pound each radish with enough force to just crush and open it slightly.
2. Crush cucumber the same way as radishes and then cut lengthwise into bite-size pieces.
3. Combine ingredients for dressing and mix well.
4. Arrange radishes and cucumber on a plate and pour dressing on just before serving.

Vermicelli Salad

4 servings
Cooking time:
15 minutes
4 ounces (100g) vermicelli
  ¼ teaspoon salt
  ½ teaspoon sesame oil
¼ stalk of celery, 1 hard-boiled egg
½ cucumber, ½ tomato
2 thick slices of ham
Dressing:
  2 tablespoons soy sauce
  6 tablespoons chicken broth
  1½ tablespoons vinegar
  2 teaspoons sugar
  1 teaspoon sesame oil

Italian dried pasta prepared with a Chinese twist makes a delightful salad.

Calories 226	Protein 16.6g	Fats 6.7g	Carbohydrates 22.4g

1. Cook vermicelli in a pot of boiling water 5 minutes. Drain well, sprinkle with salt and oil, and mix well.
2. Blanch celery until color begins to change. Rinse well in cold water and drain well.
3. Dice egg, celery, cucumber, tomato, and ham into ½-inch (1cm) cubes.
4. Combine ingredients for dressing and mix well.
5. Place vermicelli on a plate. Combine the diced ingredients and place them randomly on top of vermicelli. Pour dressing on before serving.

Salmon and Beancurd Salad

4 servings
Cooking time:
20 minutes
1 square beancurd (tofu)
4 ounces (100g) salmon
Seasoning for salmon:
  ½ teaspoon rice wine
  ¼ teaspoon salt
½ cup parsley leaves
Dressing:
  2 teaspoons dry mustard
  1 tablespoon mayonnaise
  2 tablespoons soy sauce
  ½ teaspoon vinegar
  ¼ teaspoon sugar

A pre-dinner salad that neatly combines animal and plant protein into a low-calorie feast.

Calories 136	Protein 11.4g	Fats 8.6g	Carbohydrates 2.6g

1. Place beancurd into a pot of rapidly boiling water and cook 2 minutes. Remove beancurd and drain well. Wrap it in a clean towel and wring out any excess water. Beancurd will crumble, resembling cottage cheese. Arrange beancurd on a plate.
2. Sprinkle rice wine and salt over salmon. Steam salmon about 10 minutes. Cool slightly and remove any bone and skin. Crumble salmon into flakes (photo) and set it aside to cool.
3. Blanch parsley in boiling water with salt added to it.

Remove parsley to a strainer and place it in an ice bath. Drain well any excess water and chop it coarsely.

4. Combine ingredients for dressing and mix well.

5. Arrange parsley and salmon on beancurd. Pour dressing on before serving.

Steam salmon 10 minutes and cool slightly. Crumble it into flakes, removing any bone and skin.

Crabmeat and Chicken Salad

Full consideration is given to nutritional balance as well as taste in this low-calorie pre-dinner salad.

Calories 104	Protein 9.2g	Fats 6.9g	Carbohydrates 4.0g

**4 servings
Cooking time:
25 minutes**

1. Steam chicken, spring onion, and ginger about 20 minutes. Let chicken cool slightly, and shred into long bite-size pieces.

2. Remove any cartilage from crabmeat and crumble into flakes.

3. Remove any tough string from snow peas and blanch quickly 1 to 2 minutes. Rinse them in cold water and drain well.

4. Cut mushrooms through stem and crown into 2 to 3 slices. Sprinkle them with lemon juice to keep the color.

5. Combine ingredients for dressing and mix well.

6. Spread lettuce leaves on a plate. Toss snow peas, mushrooms, chicken, and crabmeat together lightly and place them on top of lettuce. Pour dressing on before serving.

¼ teaspoon salt
1 tablespoon sesame oil

4 ounces (100g) boneless
  chicken breast
2-inch (5cm) pieces
  of spring onion
1 slice of fresh ginger
4 ounces (100g) canned
  crabmeat
12 snow peas
6 button mushrooms
1 teaspoon lemon juice
4 lettuce leaves
Dressing:
  ½ tablespoon dry mustard
  1 tablespoon vinegar
  ½ tablespoon sugar

Assorted Vegetable Salad

Ideal for health and looks.

Calories 82	Protein 7.0g	Fats 3.0g	Carbohydrates 10.2g

**4 servings
Cooking time:
30 minutes**

1. Cut cabbage into thin strips and blanch until color begins to change. Remove cabbage to a strainer and rinse well in cold water, squeeze out any excess water.

2. Cut carrot into thin strips like cabbage. Blanch 2 to 3 minutes, and follow the same procedure as cabbage.

3. Trim off both ends of bean sprouts, and blanch, again following the same procedure as

cabbage and carrot.

4. Soak dried wood-ear mushrooms in warm water until soft, then drain well.

5. Cut both cucumber and ham into strips resembling previously mentioned vegetables.

6. Combine ingredients for dressing and mix well.

7. Arrange various vegetables and ham attractively on a plate and garnish with parsley. Pour dressing on before serving.

4 ounces (100g) cabbage
4 ounces (100g) carrot
4 ounces (100g) bean sprouts
4 dried wood-ear mushrooms
4 ounces (100g) cucumber
4 thin slices of ham
Dressing:
  ½ tablespoon dry mustard
  3 tablespoons soy sauce
  1 tablespoon vinegar
  1 tablespoon sugar
  ½ tablespoon sesame oil
Garnish: Parsley

Chinese Appetizer Platters

These appetizer combinations are served around a table when entertaining guests and when drinks are served prior to the main meal. These appetizer samplings are offered in two types: Mixed Appetizer Platter (above) and A Platter of Four Cold Appetizers (below). Both consist of a well-balanced selection of meats, seafood, nuts, and vegetables.

These appetizers have been introduced to demonstrate the wide variety of Chinese appetizers, with only a sampling of these delicious appetizers introduced in this book.

Mixed Appetizer Platter

1. Jellyfish Salad with Flavorful Dressing
2. Sweet and Sour Cucumbers (recipe on page 20)
3. Steamed Chicken with Soy-Mustard Dressing
4. Smoked Whitefish
5. Cantonese Roast Pork
6. Canned Abalone
7. Soy Flavored Mushrooms (recipe on page 20)

A Platter of Four Cold Appetizers

1. Candied Walnuts
2. Abalone and Celery Salad
3. Scallops and Bean Sprouts Salad
4. Boiled Shrimp and Deep-Fried Bean Thread Noodles

Assorted Appetizers

Cold Poached Shrimp

Roast Pork

Sweet and Sour Chinese Cabbage

Soy Flavored Mushrooms

Sweet and Sour Cucumbers

Sweet and Sour Chinese Cabbage

Chinese-type pickles spiced with red peppers give this dish a bigger bite.

| Calories 48 | Protein 0.9g | Fats 2.3g | Carbohydrates 6.0g |

6 servings
Cooking time:
25 minutes
1 pound (500g) stalk sections
   of Chinese cabbage
1 teaspoon salt
Dressing:
   1 tablespoon vegetable oil
   2 dried red peppers, seeds
      removed, coarsely chopped
   3 tablespoons sugar
   3 tablespoons vinegar

1. Cut Chinese cabbage into 2-inch (5cm) strips. Sprinkle with salt and let sit 20 minutes. This will bring out the moisture in cabbage. Wring out water and place cabbage in a bowl.
2. Heat oil for dressing in a small frying pan and turn off heat. Add dried red peppers, sugar, and vinegar, and mix well.
3. Scald cabbage with hot oil and mix well. Chill before serving.

Soy Flavored Mushrooms

Use these in a combination-type appetizer. For richness in flavor, large, thick mushrooms are best.

| Calories 26 | Protein 0.3g | Fats 2.4g | Carbohydrates 0.9g |

6 servings
Cooking time:
15 minutes
12 dried mushrooms
1 tablespoon vegetable oil
1 tablespoon coarsely chopped
   spring onion
1 teaspoon julienned fresh ginger
1 tablespoon soy sauce
½ teaspoon sugar
½ cup chicken broth
¼ teaspoon sesame oil

1. Soak dried mushrooms in warm water until soft. Drain and remove stems. Cut mushrooms diagonally into 2 or 3 pieces.
2. Heat oil and add spring onion, ginger, and mushrooms. Stir-fry them briefly.
3. Add soy sauce, sugar, and chicken broth and simmer over low heat 10 minutes. Add sesame oil, and turn off heat, mix well. Cool to room temperature before serving.

Sweet and Sour Cucumbers

Pickles-in-a-jiffy flavored with garlic and sesame oil.

| Calories 37 | Protein 1.1g | Fats 2.7g | Carbohydrates 2.3g |

6 servings
Preparation
time:
10 minutes,
plus 3 hours
for pickling
8 pickling cucumbers
   1 teaspoon salt
Dressing:
   2 to 3 thin slices of garlic
   1 teaspoon sugar
   1 teaspoon salt
   2 teaspoons vinegar
   1 tablespoon sesame oil
   1 teaspoon hot bean paste
   ½ teaspoon vegetable oil

1. Cut cucumbers into quarters lengthwise, removing seeds. Cut cucumbers into 2-inch (5cm) pieces. Sprinkle salt on cucumbers and rub salt in. Keep cucumbers in a covered container 1 hour.
2. Combine ingredients for dressing and mix well.
3. When cucumbers are ready, rinse them and drain well. Pour dressing on cucumbers and marinate another 2 hours. Serve cold.

●**Cold Poached Shrimp . . . See page 12.**
●**Roast Pork . . . See page 45.**
When you prepare roast pork as an appetizer, use smaller cut of meat.

SEAFOOD DISHES

China's many lakes and rivers have made fresh-water fish about as common a food as that from the sea. Both are equally important for their protein value and, from the standpoint of health and fitness, have a comparatively lower fat and calorie content than do meats. Cod, seabass, flounder and other white-fleshed fish, as well as shrimp and shellfish, are not only low-calorie and low-fat but are also on the bland side and therefore easily fit into many and various kinds of recipes.

Scallops with Oyster Sauce
Shrimp with Chili Sauce
Shrimp with Vegetables

Steamed Butterflied Shrimp
Steamed Shrimp Cakes

Scallops with Oyster Sauce

Calories	152	Protein	15.6g	Fats	7.2g	Carbohydrates	6.2g

4 servings
Cooking time:
20 minutes
8 sea scallops
Seasoning for scallops:
  1 teaspoon rice wine
  Dash of fresh ginger juice
  1 tablespoon cornstarch
12 snow peas
4 dried mushrooms
1 ounce (25g) canned bamboo
  shoots
2 tablespoons vegetable oil
1 tablespoon coarsely
  chopped spring onion
1 teaspoon julienned fresh
  ginger
½ tablespoon rice wine

1 tablespoon oyster sauce
¼ teaspoon salt
½ teaspoon sugar

1. Slice scallops horizontally into 2 to 3 pieces. Sprinkle them with rice wine, ginger juice, and cornstarch, and mix well.
2. Remove any tough string from snow peas and blanch until color begins to change. Remove them, rinsing well in cold water, and drain.
3. Soak dried mushrooms in warm water until soft. Drain and remove stems. Cut each diago-nally into 2 to 3 pieces.
4. Slice bamboo shoots into thin strips.
5. Blanch scallops briefly in a boil, removing them before they are cooked through. Drain.
6. Heat oil and stir-fry spring onion, ginger, mushrooms, and bamboo shoots. Then add scal-lops and snow peas, and sauté them quickly. Add rice wine, oyster sauce, salt, and sugar, and stir quickly.

Shrimp with Chili Sauce

4 servings
Cooking time:
15 minutes
10 large shrimp
Seasoning for shrimp:
  ½ tablespoon rice wine
  Dash of fresh ginger juice
5 tablespoons vegetable oil
4 tablespoons coarsely chopped
  spring onion
1 clove of garlic, chopped
1 teaspoon finely julienned
  fresh ginger
3 dried red peppers, seeds
  removed, coarsely chopped
Shrimp sauce:
  2 tablespoons soy sauce
  1 tablespoon sugar
  1 teaspoon hot bean paste

¼ teaspoon salt
Twist of black pepper
3 tablespoons ketchup
1 teaspoon cornstarch dissolved
  in 2 teaspoons water
½ teaspoon sesame oil

One of the most representative Chinese dishes. For best results use large shrimp and cook them in the shell for maximum flavor retention.

Calories	254	Protein	12.4g	Fats	17.2g	Carbohydrates	10.6g

1. Devein shrimp and trim off only the legs.
2. Cut shrimp into 3 pieces each. Sprinkle them with rice wine and ginger juice, and mix well.
3. Combine ingredients for shrimp sauce and mix well.
4. Heat oil and sauté shrimp over high heat. When color of shrimp begins to change, add spring onion, garlic, ginger, and red peppers. Add sauce and stir-fry until fragrance of shrimp and sauce is released.
5. Add dissolved cornstarch and stir quickly until sauce thi-ckens. Add sesame oil, turn off heat, and mix well.

Shrimp with Vegetables

4 servings
Cooking time:
20 minutes
½ pound (250g) shrimp
Seasoning for shrimp:

Shrimp needs pre-seasoning and cooks fast, so cook the vegetables and shrimp separately.

Calories	144	Protein	9.6g	Fats	10.3g	Carbohydrates	2.3g

1. Shell and devein shrimp. Sprinkle with rice wine, ginger juice, and cornstarch, and mix well.

2. Remove any tough string from snow peas and blanch them in boiling water. Drain quickly and rinse in running water. Drain well.
3. Remove strings from celery and slice diagonally into thin strips.
4. Cut mushrooms through stem and crown into 2 to 3 slices.
5. Heat 1 tablespoon of oil and stir-fry celery, mushrooms, and snow peas slightly. Remove to a dish and reserve.
6. Heat 2 tablespoons of oil and stir-fry shrimp briefly. Return vegetables to shrimp, adding rice wine, salt and sugar, and stir again.

1 teaspoon rice wine
½ teaspoon fresh ginger juice
1 teaspoon cornstarch
12 snow peas
1 stalk celery
6 button mushrooms
3 tablespoons vegetable oil
1 tablespoon rice wine
1 teaspoon salt
1 teaspoon sugar

Steamed Butterflied Shrimp

Calories 104	Protein 12.7g	Fats 3.9g	Carbohydrates 4.7g

1. Shell shrimp, being careful to leave tails on. Devein and butterfly them. Pierce a small hole in the middle of each opened shrimp. Sprinkle with seasoning and mix well.
2. Place a few strips of bamboo shoots and ham near the tail section of shrimp. Fold the tail so that you can pull it through the hole, forming a rolled shrimp which looks like a blossoming flower.
3. Place the rolled shrimp on a plate in a steamer and steam about 10 minutes.
4. Cut spinach into 2-inch (5cm) lengths. Heat oil, add salt, and quickly stir-fry spinach. Add sugar and water and stir again. Drain any dark liquid before arranging spinach on a plate.
5. Combine chicken broth, salt, and sugar for sauce, and bring to a boil. Add dissolved cornstarch and quickly stir until sauce thickens.
6. Arrange shrimp on spinach and pour the sauce over before serving.

½ cup chicken broth
¼ teaspoon salt
¼ teaspoon sugar
½ teaspoon cornstarch dissolved in 1 teaspoon water

4 servings
Cooking time:
40 minutes

8 medium-size shrimp
Seasoning for shrimp:
　Dash of rice wine
　Pinch of salt
　Dash of fresh ginger juice
4 ounces (100g) canned bamboo shoots, julienned into 2-inch (5cm) lengths
1 thin slice of ham, cut into 2-inch (5cm) strips
½ pound (250g) spinach
1 tablespoon vegetable oil
Pinch of salt
¼ teaspoon sugar
1 tablespoon water
Light sauce:

Steamed Shrimp Cakes

Calories 123	Protein 13.9g	Fats 4.7g	Carbohydrates 4.7g

1. Shell and devein shrimp, then purée in a food processor. Combine the puréed shrimp, water chestnuts, rice wine, salt, and ginger juice in a bowl. Gradually add water, mixing well. Add egg white and sprinkle with cornstarch, again mixing well.
2. Cut ham into 12 slices 2-inch (5cm) in diameter.
3. Sprinkle a little cornstarch on each slice of ham. Divide shrimp purée into 12 portions and place a portion on each slice of ham. Place the 12 shrimp cakes on a plate which fits into a steamer.
4. Place the plate of shrimp cakes in the steamer and steam 10 minutes.
5. Cut asparagus into diagonal slices. Heat oil before adding salt and sugar, and stir-fry asparagus over high heat until tender.
6. Combine chicken broth, salt, and sugar, and bring to a boil. Add dissolved cornstarch and quickly stir until sauce thickens.
7. Arrange shrimp cakes and asparagus on the plate and nap with sauce before serving.

½ teaspoon salt
½ teaspoon sugar
½ teaspoon cornstarch dissolved in 1 teaspoon water

4 servings
Cooking time:
40 minutes

½ pound (250g) shrimp
2 canned water chestnuts, finely chopped
1 teaspoon rice wine
½ teaspoon salt
½ teaspoon fresh ginger juice
2 to 3 tablespoons water
½ egg white
1 tablespoon cornstarch
6 to 7 thin slices of ham
Cornstarch for dusting
6 spears fresh asparagus
1 tablespoon vegetable oil
Pinch of salt
Pinch of sugar
Light sauce:
　½ cup chicken broth

Fried Breaded Shrimp Balls

Oyster Puffs

Sweet and Sour Shrimp

Fish Toast with Ham

Fried Breaded Shrimp Balls

4 servings
Cooking time:
30 minutes
½ pound (250g) shrimp
3 slices of white bread, ¼-inch (0.5cm) thick
1 tablespoon rice wine
1 tablespoon fresh ginger juice
1 teaspoon salt
⅓ cup water
1 egg white
2 tablespoons cornstarch
3 to 4 cups oil for deep-frying

A crispy-tasty specialty. Like the Shrimp Toast on page 10 the oil temperature is the key to success.

| Calories 175 | Protein 10.6g | Fats 9.8g | Carbohydrates 9.4g |

1. Shell and devein shrimp (photo A), then purée in a food processor or blender.
2. Cut off crusts from bread and slice into ¼-inch (0.5cm) cubes.
3. Place the puréed shrimp in a bowl and add rice wine, ginger juice, and salt, mixing well. Gradually add water, mixing well. Add egg white and mix well. Finally, gradually sprinkle cornstarch and mix well (photo B).
4. Spread bread cubes on a tray or some wax paper. Divide puréed shrimp into equal portions and roll them into 1 to 1½-inch (2.5 to 3cm) balls. Drop them onto bread cubes and roll them to make an even layer of bread cubes on each ball (photo C).
5. Heat oil for deep-frying to 340° F (170°C) and deep-fry shrimp balls until golden brown and cooked to the center. Remove them from the wok with a strainer, drain them well, and serve while still hot.

A. Shell and devein shrimp using a toothpick to remove vein, and purée in a food processor.

B. Add seasoning, water, egg white, and cornstarch to puréed shrimp and mix well.

C. Roll shrimp balls to make an even layer of bread cubes on each ball.

Oyster Puffs

4 servings
Cooking time:
20 minutes
6 ounces (150g) oysters, shucked
Batter:
  ¾ cup all-purpose flour
  ¼ cup cornstarch
  1 teaspoon baking powder
  Pinch of salt
  ½ cup water, plus 2 to 3 tablespoons
  1 tablespoon vegetable oil
3 to 4 cups oil for deep-frying
Garnish:
  Parsley

Briefly blanch the oysters before deep-frying to remove most of the excess water. Blanching or frying too long will make them tough and lose their flavor.

| Calories 367 | Protein 5.2g | Fats 27.9g | Carbohydrates 21.1g |

1. Place oysters in a colander and sprinkle them with a little salt. Wash them gently and drain. Blanch them 1 minute. Remove and drain once more until nearly dry. Absorb any remaining water from oysters with paper towels or a cloth.
2. Combine all dry ingredients for batter in a bowl and mix well, adding water and oil gradually.
3. Heat oil for deep-frying to 340°F (170°C). Dip oysters into batter and drop them gently into the oil. Deep-fry until golden brown. Drain well.
4. Arrange oysters on a plate. Garnish with some parsley and serve while still hot.

Sweet and Sour Shrimp

Choose medium-to-large shrimp. Cooking them in the shell helps lock in the flavor.

Calories 161	Protein 9.8g	Fats 10.1g	Carbohydrates 5.8g

**4 servings
Cooking time:
15 minutes**

8 large shrimp
3 tablespoons vegetable oil
1 teaspoon coarsely chopped
   spring onion
1 teaspoon coarsely chopped
   fresh ginger
1 tablespoon rice wine
2 tablespoons sugar
2 tablespoons soy sauce
1½ tablespoons vinegar
¼ teaspoon cornstarch
   dissolved in ½ teaspoon
   water
Garnish:
   Parsley

1. Devein shrimp and trim off only the legs. Pat them dry with paper towels or a cloth. As an option, you may cut shrimp in half, as this will allow them to absorb flavor of sauce better. This is recommended for larger sized shrimp.
2. Heat oil and sauté shrimp over high heat. When color of shrimp begins to change, stir-fry spring onion and ginger briefly. Add rice wine, sugar, soy sauce, and vinegar, and stir quickly.
3. Add dissolved cornstarch and stir quickly until sauce thickens.
4. Arrange shrimp on a plate. Garnish with parsley and serve while still hot.

Fish Toast with Ham

To help keep the calories low, use white-fleshed fish and make boneless ham your choice of meat. As in all recipes that call for toast, remember that the crispness is obtained through careful control of the oil temperature.

Calories 173	Protein 10.6g	Fats 10.0g	Carbohydrates 8.7g

**4 servings
Cooking time:
20 minutes**

3 slices white bread, ¼-inch
   (0.5cm) thick
6 ounces (150g) whitefish (cod,
   sea bass, or flounder)
Seasoning for fish:
   1 teaspoon rice wine
   ½ teaspoon fresh ginger juice
   ½ teaspoon salt
3 thin slices of ham
1 egg
1½ tablespoons cornstarch
Cornstarch for dusting
3 to 4 cups oil for deep-frying

1. Cut off crusts from bread and cut into quarters.
2. Slice fish into 12 thin pieces and trim them to the same size as bread. Sprinkle fish with rice wine, ginger juice, and salt, and mix well.
3. Cut ham into 12 pieces the same size and shape as bread.
4. Beat egg lightly and add 1½ tablespoons of cornstarch gradually as you beat the egg.
5. Sprinkle some cornstarch on the surface of bread. Dip fish individually into the egg mixture and place on bread. Place ham on top of the fish. Repeat this for all 12 pieces (photo).
6. Heat oil for deep-frying to 340°F (170°C). Gently drop fish toast with fish side down into the oil. Deep-fry them until golden brown. Remove and drain well. Arrange on a plate and serve while still hot.

Place fish dipped into the egg mixture on bread. Place ham on top of the fish.

Steamed Whitefish with Ham and Mushrooms

Abalone and Cauliflower in Mock Cream Sauce

Steamed Whitefish with Ham and Mushrooms

4 servings
Cooking time:
30 minutes

½ pound (250g) whitefish
(cod, sea bass or flounder)
Seasoning for fish:
1 teaspoon rice wine
½ teaspoon salt
¼ teaspoon sugar
Twist of pepper
½ tablespoon cornstarch
4 thin slices of ham
6 dried mushrooms
Vegetable oil for brushing
Light sauce:
½ cup chicken broth
1 tablespoon vegetable oil
¼ teaspoon salt
¼ teaspoon sugar
¼ teaspoon sesame oil
½ teaspoon cornstarch
dissolved in 1 teaspoon water

Steaming is a common style of Chinese cooking. It prevents loss of precious nutrients, helps to seal in flavors, and is, at the same time, an ideal way to cook for a low-calorie, low-fat meal.

Calories 102	Protein 13.6g	Fats 4.5g	Carbohydrates 4.0g

1. Slice fish into 12 thin pieces. Sprinkle them with rice wine, salt, sugar, pepper, and cornstarch, and mix well.
2. Cut ham into 12 pieces, the same size as fish.
3. Soak dried mushrooms in warm water, and remove stems. Cut diagonally into 12 slices.
4. Combine 1 slice each of ham, fish, and mushroom so that you will have 12 packages (photo).
5. Brush a dish with a little vegetable oil, and arrange the 12 packages into 2 rows.
6. Place the dish in a steamer and steam about 8 minutes.
7. Combine chicken broth, oil, salt, sugar, and sesame oil, and

bring to a boil. Add dissolved cornstarch and stir quickly until sauce thickens.
8. Nap fish with sauce. You may rearrange fish on a plate when serving, or serve it directly from the steamer.

Combine 1 slice each of ham, fish, and mushroom together. Repeat 12 times.

Abalone with Cauliflower in Mock Cream Sauce

4 servings
Cooking time:
15 minutes

4 ounces (100g) canned abalone
½ head cauliflower
8 pieces canned baby corn
1 tablespoon vegetable oil
3 ounces (80g) canned whole
mushrooms
½ cup chicken broth
1 cup milk
½ teaspoon sugar
2 teaspoons salt
1½ tablespoons cornstarch
dissolved in 2 tablespoons
water

Canned rather than fresh abalone gives the best results. There is a special, unique flavor about canned abalone that is unmatched by the fresh. Moreover, canned abalone is much more tender.

Calories 112	Protein 8.7g	Fats 5.2g	Carbohydrates 8.5g

1. Slice abalone into thin pieces.
2. Cut cauliflower into small flowerettes and cook in rapidly boiling water 2 to 3 minutes or until tender.
3. Cut baby corn in half, lengthwise.
4. Heat oil and quickly stir-fry

abalone, cauliflower, baby corn and mushrooms. Add chicken broth.
5. When chicken broth comes to a boil, add milk, sugar, and salt, and bring to a second boil. Add dissolved cornstarch and stir quickly until sauce thickens.

MEAT DISHES

Although meats of various kinds are used for food in China, pork is probably the most common and is generally what is meant by the word "meat." Other meats often eaten are beef, chicken and duck.

Meats, however, as compared with seafood and vegetables, are heavier in fat content and tend to have a higher calorie count, although that will vary according to the cut or section. Pork and beef, for example, increase in both fat and calories as the cuts go from the tougher to the more tender portions, and the fatty skin of chicken is especially high in calories. Nevertheless, for the sake of their high-quality protein, meats should not be eliminated from the diet but simply controlled as to volume and frequency of intake.

Tomato Beef
Chinese Beefsteak
Mongolian Beef

Beef with Celery and Carrot
Beef with Green Bell Peppers

Tomato Beef

Calories 209	Protein 14.3g	Fats 13.7g	Carbohydrates 5.4g

4 servings
Cooking time:
15 minutes
½ pound (250g) lean beef,
  thinly sliced
Seasoning for beef:
  1 teaspoon rice wine
  1 teaspoon soy sauce
  1 teaspoon cornstarch
2 ripe tomatoes
3 tablespoons vegetable oil
2 tablespoons coarsely
  chopped spring onion

1 teaspoon julienned fresh
  ginger
1 teaspoon rice wine
½ teaspoon salt
Pinch of sugar
1 teaspoon soy sauce

1. Cut beef into 2-inch (5cm) pieces. Sprinkle the pieces with rice wine, soy sauce, and cornstarch, mixing them lightly.
2. Cut tomatoes into 8 wedges, removing seeds.
3. Heat 1 tablespoon of oil and stir-fry tomatoes quickly over high heat. Remove to a dish and reserve.
4. Heat 2 tablespoons of oil and add spring onion, ginger, and beef, stirring until color of meat begins to change. Return tomatoes to the wok with beef, adding rice wine, salt, sugar, and soy sauce, and stir again.

Chinese Beefsteak

The sauce and the pre-seasoning of the meat make this dish interestingly different from the western-style steak.

Calories 245	Protein 27.1g	Fats 11.4g	Carbohydrates 5.4g

4 servings
Cooking time:
10 minutes,
plus 10 minutes
for marinating
4 medium pieces of steak rump
Seasoning for steak:
  1 tablespoon rice wine
  1 teaspoon sugar
  1 teaspoon soy sauce
  ½ teaspoon salt
  ½ teaspoon sesame oil
  Twist of black pepper
  2 teaspoons cornstarch
Sauce:
  ½ tablespoon ketchup
  1 tablespoon Worcestershire

sauce
  1 tablespoon soy sauce
  1 teaspoon sugar
1 tablespoon vegetable oil
Garnish:
  Lemon, parsley

1. Pound steak lightly with blunt edge of knife. Sprinkle steak with seasoning and mix well. Allow beef to sit about 10 minutes.
2. Combine ingredients for sauce and mix well.
3. Heat oil and sauté on both sides to the degree you desire. Add sauce and quickly turn the steak once more so that it absorbs the flavor of sauce.
4. Cut the steak into large bite-size pieces and arrange on a plate. Garnish with lemon and parsley.

Mongolian Beef

Calories 237	Protein 14.3g	Fats 17.2g	Carbohydrates 3.4g

4 servings
Cooking time:
15 minutes
½ pound (250g) lean beef,
  thinly sliced
Seasoning for beef:
  1½ tablespoons vegetable oil
  1½ tablespoons rice wine
  2 teaspoons soy sauce
  Twist of black pepper
2 whole spring onions
Sauce:
  2 teaspoons soy sauce
  2 teaspoons vinegar

2 teaspoons sesame oil
¼ teaspoon salt
2 tablespoons vegetable oil
1 clove of garlic, thinly
  sliced

1. Cut beef into 2-inch (5cm) pieces and sprinkle with oil, rice wine, soy sauce, and pepper, and mix lightly.
2. Cut spring onions diagonally into ½-inch (1cm) thick slices.
3. Combine ingredients for sauce and mix well.
4. Heat oil and stir-fry garlic until flavor is released. Add beef, at the same time turning heat to high and stir quickly. Add spring onions and stir again. When spring onions have become soft, add sauce and stir again until all ingredients are mixed well.

Beef with Celery and Carrot

A pan-fried dish that derives its excellence from the fragrance and crunchiness of the celery.

Calories 203	Protein 14.5g	Fats 13.6g	Carbohydrates 3.7g

4 servings
Cooking time:
25 minutes

1. Cut beef into 2-inch (5cm) strips the size of pencil. Sprinkle them with rice wine, soy sauce, and ginger juice and mix lightly.
2. Remove strings from celery and peel carrot. Julienne both into 2-inch (5cm) lengths.
3. Remove stem and seeds from dried red pepper and chop it coarsely.
4. Heat 1 tablespoon of oil and stir-fry celery and carrot slightly. Remove to a dish and reserve.
5. Heat the remaining 2 tablespoons of oil. Stir-fry spring onion, ginger, and red pepper slightly. Add beef and stir again quickly. When color of beef begins to change, add soy sauce, sugar, and pepper.
6. Finally, return celery and carrot to beef, and stir thoroughly.

½ pound (250g) lean beef, thinly sliced
Seasoning for beef:
　1 teaspoon rice wine
　1 tablespoon soy sauce
　½ teaspoon fresh ginger juice
1 stalk of celery
4 ounces (100g) carrot
1 dried red pepper
3 tablespoons vegetable oil
2 teaspoons coarsely chopped spring onion
1 teaspoon julienned fresh ginger
1 tablespoon soy sauce
½ teaspoon sugar
Twist of black pepper

Beef with Green Bell Peppers

This is one of the most popular stir-fried dishes in all of Chinese cooking.

Calories 261	Protein 14.3g	Fats 20.1g	Carbohydrates 3.7g

4 servings
Cooking time:
25 minutes

1. Cut beef into 2-inch (5cm) strips the size of pencil (photo A). Sprinkle them with rice wine, soy sauce, and cornstarch, and mix lightly (photo B).
2. Cut green bell peppers into strips the same size as beef (photo C).
3. Heat 2 tablespoons of oil, adding a pinch of salt and quickly stir-fry the green bell peppers. Remove to a dish and reserve.
4. Heat the remaining 3 tablespoons of oil. Stir-fry spring onion, ginger, and garlic lightly, add beef, and stir until color begins to change. Add soy sauce, salt, and sugar and stir again.
5. Finally, return green peppers to beef, and stir again thoroughly.

½ pound (250g) lean beef, thinly sliced
Seasoning for beef:
　1 teaspoon rice wine
　½ tablespoon soy sauce
　1 tablespoon cornstarch
5 green bell peppers
5 tablespoons vegetable oil
Pinch of salt
1 tablespoon coarsely chopped spring onion
1 teaspoon coarsely chopped fresh ginger
1 clove of garlic, coarsely chopped
1 tablespoon soy sauce
½ teaspoon salt
½ teaspoon sugar

A. Cut beef across the grain into 2-inch (5cm) strips the size of pencil.

B. Sprinkle rice wine, soy sauce, and cornstarch on beef and mix lightly.

C. Cut green bell peppers each in half and remove seeds. Cut into strips the same size as beef.

Curried Beef with Onions

Stewed Beef with Carrots

Ground Pork in Bamboo

Braised Meatballs

Curried Beef with Onions

4 servings
Cooking time:
1 hour
40 minutes

1 pound (500g) stewing beef
5 tablespoons vegetable oil
1 clove of garlic, thinly
  sliced
8 to 10 small onions, peeled
2 ounces (50g) canned whole
  mushrooms
1 tablespoon curry powder
2 tablespoons rice wine
6 tablespoons soy sauce
½ tablespoon sugar

Cuts of beef especially suited for simmered dishes include shoulder, round and neck. The simmering breaks down the connective tissue that causes the toughness. These cuts are also lean and thus ideal for health and fitness.

Calories 380	Protein 29.8g	Fats 24.2g	Carbohydrates 8.8g

1. Cut beef into bite-size pieces.

2. Heat 3 tablespoons of oil in a stewing pot and stir-fry beef until browned on all sides. Add water to cover beef and bring to a boil, remembering to skim off as much foam as possible. Lower heat and simmer beef 1 hour or until tender.

3. Heat the remaining 2 tablespoons of oil. Add garlic, onions, and mushrooms, and stir quickly. Add curry powder and mix well. Add rice wine, soy sauce, and sugar and mix well.

4. Add curry mixture to simmering beef and simmer another 20 minutes.

Stewed Beef with Carrots

4 servings
Cooking time:
1 hour
40 minutes

1 pound (500g) stewing beef
3 tablespoons vegetable oil
4 tablespoons coarsely chopped
  spring onion
1 teaspoon coarsely chopped
  fresh ginger
1 clove of garlic, coarsely
  chopped
1 tablespoon rice wine
5 tablespoons soy sauce
½ tablespoon sugar
2 carrots
2 potatoes

This traditional stew is an excellent example of down-home Chinese cooking. At first glance—but not taste!—it may appear little different from a western-style stew, as both contain the essentials of beef, carrots and potatoes. The difference lies in the soy sauce flavoring.

Calories 372	Protein 30.7g	Fats 17.7g	Carbohydrates 19.0g

1. Cut beef into bite-size pieces.

2. Heat 2 tablespoons of oil in a stewing pot and stir-fry spring onion, ginger, and garlic lightly. Add beef and stir again until browned on all sides. Add rice wine, soy sauce, and sugar, and water to cover. Bring to a rapid boil and skim off as much foam as possible. Lower heat and simmer beef 1 hour or until tender.

3. Peel carrots and cut into bite-size pieces (photo).

4. Peel potatoes and cut into bite-size pieces, and soak in cold water about 5 minutes.

5. Heat the remaining 1 tablespoon of oil and stir-fry carrots and potatoes lightly.

6. Add carrots and potatoes to simmering beef and simmer another 30 minutes or until vegetables are tender.

Peel carrots and cut diagonally but alternating directions into slightly triangular shaped pieces.

Ground Pork in Bamboo

To allow the flavor of the bamboo to seep into the meat and impart its exotic taste, it is best to use a container made from bamboo. If unavailable, then a Pyrex cup or a ceramic custard cup will serve the purpose. Even a coffee cup will do.

Calories	63	Protein	8.1g	Fats	2.8g	Carbohydrates	0.7g

**4 servings
Cooking time:
30 minutes**

6 ounces (150g) ground pork
1 cup water
1 ounce (25g) canned bamboo shoots, finely chopped
1 teaspoon finely chopped spring onion
Seasoning for ground pork:
　1 teaspoon light soy sauce
　½ tablespoon soy sauce
　½ teaspoon salt

1. Place ground pork in a food processor or blender. Add water, bamboo shoots, spring onion, and seasoning ingredients. Purée until smooth.
2. Divide puréed pork evenly into four containers they are to be steamed in (photo).
3. Place four containers in a steamer over high heat. Steam about 20 minutes.
4. Remove containers from the steamer and serve them on small saucers, while still hot.
Note: If you do not have a steamer, you may also use the oven by filling a shallow baking dish with water and placing the containers in it.

Put puréed pork evenly into four bamboo containers.

Braised Meatballs

The Chinese name for this dish is "Lion's Head", since the large-sized meatballs resemble the majestic head of a lion. It can be served in a deep dish as shown in the photo, or cooked in a casserole and brought directly to the table.

Calories	455	Protein	27.5g	Fats	33.0g	Carbohydrates	8.1g

**4 servings
Cooking time:
50 minutes**

1 pound (500g) ground pork
Seasoning for ground pork:
　1 tablespoon rice wine
　½ tablespoon soy sauce
　Pinch of salt
　3 tablespoons water
　3 tablespoons finely chopped spring onion
　1 teaspoon fresh ginger juice
　1 egg
　1 tablespoon cornstarch
1 pound (500g) Chinese green cabbage or Chinese cabbage
4 dried mushrooms
1 small canned bamboo shoots
2 tablespoons vegetable oil
1½ cups chicken broth
2 tablespoons rice wine
½ teaspoon soy sauce
½ teaspoon salt
½ teaspoon sugar

1. Combine ground pork with rice wine, soy sauce, salt, water, spring onion, ginger juice, and egg in a bowl and mix thoroughly. Add cornstarch and mix again until well blended.
2. Divide meat mixture into 4 equal portions. Make meatballs with greased hands.
3. Cut Chinese green cabbage into small squares.
4. Soak dried mushrooms in warm water until soft. Remove stems and slice in half diagonally.
5. Cut bamboo shoots into thin slices.
6. Heat 1 tablespoon of oil and sauté meatballs until browned on all sides. Remove to a dish and reserve.
7. Heat chicken broth in a casserole and place meatballs in broth and cover the casserole. Cook meatballs 30 minutes.
8. Heat the remaining 1 tablespoon of oil and stir-fry mushrooms, bamboo shoots, and Chinese green cabbage.
9. Add stir-fried vegetables to meatballs, adding rice wine, soy sauce, salt, and sugar. Simmer until vegetables are tender.
Note: To make sure there are no air bubbles trapped in the meatball, gently toss the meatball back and forth in your hands. If air becomes trapped in the meatballs, this will cause them to break while cooking.

Stewed Chicken with Onions
Chicken with Garden Vegetables
Chicken with Oyster Sauce

Chinese Fried Chicken
Spiced Soy Sauce Chicken

Stewed Chicken with Onions

Calories	392	Protein	30.6g	Fats	25.1g	Carbohydrates	7.6g

4 servings
Cooking time:
1 hour
15 minutes
1½ pounds (750g) chicken parts
2 tablespoons soy sauce
3 tablespoons vegetable oil
12 small onions, peeled
2 ounces (50g) canned whole
   mushrooms
½ teaspoon salt
3 slices of fresh ginger
1 small clove of garlic,
   finely chopped
2 tablespoons finely
   chopped zha cai

1. Using a cleaver, cut chicken into bite-size pieces, leaving in the bones. Sprinkle soy sauce on chicken pieces and let stand about 10 minutes.
2. Heat 2 tablespoons of oil in a stewing pot. Stir-fry onions, mushrooms, and salt until onions turn golden brown. Remove from the pot and reserve.

1 tablespoon rice wine
2 tablespoons soy sauce
1 tablespoon sugar

3. Heat the remaining 1 tablespoon of oil in the pot until hot and stir-fry chicken until color changes. Add ginger, garlic, zha cai, rice wine, and soy sauce and stir all ingredients well. Add some water to cover and sugar. Bring this to a boil, and lower heat. Cover the pot and simmer about 40 minutes.
4. When chicken is done, add onions and cook another 20 minutes at a low simmer.

Chicken with Garden Vegetables

Calories	173	Protein	8.1g	Fats	12.9g	Carbohydrates	4.2g

4 servings
Cooking time:
25 minutes
6 ounces (150g) boneless
   chicken breast
Seasoning for chicken:
   1 teaspoon rice wine
   ½ teaspoon fresh ginger juice
   ½ teaspoon cornstarch
1 ounce (25g) carrot
8 snow peas
1 green bell pepper
1 red bell pepper
½ stalk celery
4 pieces canned baby corn
2 tablespoons vegetable oil
1 teaspoon coarsely chopped
   spring onion

1. Cut chicken into thin slices. Sprinkle them with rice wine and ginger juice and mix well. Add cornstarch and mix well.
2. Cut carrot into thin slices. Blanch them quickly and rinse in cold water. Drain well.
3. Remove any tough string from the snow peas and blanch quickly. Rinse with cold water and drain well.
4. Cut green and red bell pep-

1 tablespoon rice wine
1 teaspoon salt
1 teaspoon sugar

pers into 8 pieces. Remove any string from celery and cut into thin slices diagonally. Cut baby corn lengthwise in half.
5. Heat 1 tablespoon of oil and stir-fry green and red bell peppers, celery, carrot, corn, and snow peas. Remove to a dish and reserve.
6. Heat 1 tablespoon of oil and stir-fry spring onion slightly. Add chicken and stir until color changes. Return vegetables to the wok and season with rice wine, salt, and sugar, mixing ingredients well.

Chicken with Oyster Sauce

Calories	338	Protein	15.8g	Fats	26.4g	Carbohydrates	6.2g

4 servings
Cooking time:
20 minutes
10 ounces (300g) boneless
   chicken breast
Seasoning for chicken:
   ½ tablespoon rice wine
   ½ tablespoon soy sauce
   Twist of black pepper
   1 tablespoon cornstarch

1. Cut chicken into thick slices diagonally. Sprinkle chicken with rice wine, soy sauce, and pepper. Add cornstarch and mix well.
2. Slice asparagus diagonally also into bite-size pieces.
3. Heat 1 tablespoon of oil, add pinch of salt, and stir-fry aspar-

agus quickly. Arrange on a serving plate.
4. Heat 2 more tablespoons of oil and sauté chicken on both sides until slightly gold. Remove to a dish.
5. Heat the remaining 1 tablespoon of oil and stir-fry ginger

and garlic lightly. Return chicken and add oyster sauce, soy sauce, and sesame oil and stir again.
6. Arrange chicken on top of asparagus.

chopped
2 tablespoons oyster sauce
1 teaspoon soy sauce
1 teaspoon sesame oil

8 spears fresh asparagus
4 tablespoons vegetable oil
1 teaspoon finely chopped fresh ginger
1 small clove of garlic, finely

Chinese Fried Chicken

Calories 398	Protein 21.0g	Fats 29.1g	Carbohydrates 8.6g

**4 servings
Cooking time:
10 minutes,
plus 30 minutes
for marinating**

1. Combine soy sauce, rice wine, and ginger juice and marinate drumsticks in it 30 minutes. When 30 minutes is over, drain chicken well, and sprinkle chicken evenly with cornstarch.
2. Heat oil for deep-frying to 360°F (180°C) and deep-fry drumsticks until cooked to the center and golden brown.
3. Garnish the pieces with watercress and lemon when serving.

4 to 5 tablespoons cornstarch
3 to 4 cups oil for deep-frying
Garnish: Watercress, lemon

8 chicken drumsticks
Seasoning for drumsticks:
  2 tablespoons soy sauce
  1 tablespoon rice wine
  ½ teaspoon fresh ginger
  juice

Spiced Soy Sauce Chicken

Calories 259	Protein 20.1g	Fats 13.2g	Carbohydrates 10.3g

**8 servings
Cooking time:
35 minutes**

1. Place all ingredients for sauce in a stewing pot and bring to a boil. Add chicken and simmer about 15 to 20 minutes, remembering to turn chicken several times so that it is cooked evenly on both sides. Turn off heat and allow chicken to steep in sauce 10 minutes with lid closed.
2. Remove chicken from the pot and coat with sesame oil on both sides.
3. When chicken is cool, cut into bite-size pieces.
4. Arrange chicken on a plate and garnish with cilantro.

1 star anise
1 tablespoon sesame oil
Garnish: Cilantro

2 pieces chicken thigh and leg with bone
2 pieces whole chicken breast with bone
Sauce:
  1½ cups soy sauce
  ½ cup rice wine
  ½ cup water
  4 tablespoons brown sugar

Roast Pork   (see photo on page 47)

Calories 209	Protein 21.4g	Fats 8.6g	Carbohydrates 7.7g

**8 servings
Cooking time:
1 hour, plus
4 to 5 hours
for marinating**

1. Tie pork roast with string, and pierce pork in several places with a skewer to allow marinade to seep into meat.
2. Combine ingredients for marinade well and pour over pork. Marinate 4 to 5 hours, remembering to turn occasionally.
3. Preheat an oven to 360°F (180° C). Place pork on top of a rack and place the rack in a roasting pan. Brush pork lightly with vegetable oil and pour 1 to 2 tablespoons of marinade over it. Roast about 1 hour or until the center is cooked, occasionally basting with marinade. To test when pork is done, pierce meat with the skewer. If juice is clear and not pink, roast is done. You may also use meat thermometer.
4. Slice roast into ¼-inch (0.5cm) slices and arrange pieces on a plate. Garnish with spring onion and cilantro.

1½ pounds (750g) boneless pork loin roast
Marinade for pork:
  1 cup soy sauce
  5 tablespoons rice wine
  4 tablespoons sugar
  1 tablespoon salt
  4 slices fresh ginger
  1 star anise
1 tablespoon vegetable oil
Garnish: Spring onion, cilantro

Sweet and Sour Pork

Roast Pork
Pork with Oyster Sauce

Sweet and Sour Pork

4 servings
Cooking time:
45 minutes
½ pound (250g) lean pork
tenderloin
Seasoning for pork:
1 teaspoon soy sauce
1 teaspoon rice wine
½ teaspoon fresh ginger
juice
1½ tablespoons cornstarch
2 dried mushrooms
½ medium onion
1 green bell pepper
1 ounce (25g) canned bamboo
shoots
2 ounces (50g) carrot
3 to 4 cups oil for deep-frying
2 tablespoons vegetable oil
1 clove of garlic, finely
chopped
Sauce:
½ cup chicken broth
5 tablespoons sugar
1½ tablespoons soy sauce
1 tablespoon ketchup
½ teaspoon salt

1 tablespoon cornstarch
dissolved in 2 tablespoons
water
4 tablespoons vinegar
2 slices canned pineapple,
cut into 6 pieces

Along with Beef with Green Bell Peppers on page 35 this dish is one of the most popular Chinese foods enjoyed by people around the world.

| Calories 285 | Protein 15.5g | Fats 13.2g | Carbohydrates 25.4g |

1. Cut pork into bite-size squares. Combine soy sauce, rice wine, and ginger juice and marinate pork in it 15 minutes. Wait until you are ready to cook it before adding cornstarch.
2. Soak dried mushrooms in warm water until soft and remove stems. Cut into thin slices.
3. Slice onion into bite-size pieces. Cut bell pepper as onion. Cut bamboo shoots into thin slices.
4. Slice carrot into thin rounds and parboil. Rinse with cold water and drain.
5. Heat oil for deep-frying to 360°F (180°C). Deep-fry pork until golden brown. Remove from the wok and drain.
6. Heat 2 tablespoons of vegetable oil. Stir-fry garlic and add vegetables in the following order: mushrooms, onion, bamboo shoots, bell pepper, and carrot.
7. Combine chicken broth, sugar, soy sauce, ketchup, and salt and add this to vegetables. Bring this sauce to a boil and mix in dissolved cornstarch quickly, stirring constantly. When sauce is thickened, add vinegar and pork. Add pineapple last and stir well before serving.

Pork with Oyster Sauce

4 servings
Cooking time:
20 minutes
½ pound (250g) lean pork
tenderloin, thinly sliced
Seasoning for pork:
½ teaspoon rice wine
¼ teaspoon soy sauce
½ teaspoon sugar
½ teaspoon sesame oil
Pinch of salt
Twist of black pepper
1 egg yolk
1 tablespoon cornstarch
½ pound (250g) spinach
3 tablespoons vegetable oil
½ teaspoon salt
¼ teaspoon sugar
1 tablespoon water
2 tablespoons oyster sauce
½ teaspoon sesame oil
Twist of black pepper

Pork tenderloin is low in fat. The oyster sauce in the recipe gives the meat a very special flavor that differs considerably from that found in Sweet and Sour Pork.

| Calories 233 | Protein 16.3g | Fats 14.9g | Carbohydrates 7.2g |

1. Slice pork into bite-size pieces. Combine rice wine, soy sauce, sugar, sesame oil, salt, pepper, and egg yolk and mix well. Marinate pork in this sauce. Wait until you are ready to cook before adding cornstarch.
2. Cut spinach into 2-inch (5cm) lengths. Heat 1 tablespoon of oil. Add salt and spinach and quickly stir-fry. Add sugar and water and stir again. Drain dark liquid before arrang-ing spinach on a plate.
3. Heat the remaining 2 tablespoons of oil and sauté pork until golden brown on both sides. Remove pork from the wok and reserve.
4. Add oyster sauce to the wok and when it begins to bubble, return pork to the wok and stir-fry briskly. Sprinkle with sesame oil and pepper and stir again.
5. Arrange pork on top of spinach and serve.

●Roast Pork...See page 45

VEGETABLE DISHES

Vegetables contain such essential vitamins as the A in carotene and Vitamin C, provide fiber, and are a necessary food for health and fitness. They are, in general, highly compatible with oil, since the carotene in them is an oil-soluble vitamin and the oil thus aids in its absorption. Even so, too much oil can lead to too many calories, and for that reason careful consideration has been given to keeping the amount of oil to an absolute minimum in the vegetable dishes that appear on the following pages.

Szechuan Pickled Vegetables
Chilled Celery with Mustard
Eggplants with Soy Dressing

Sautéed Eggplants
Sautéed Tomatoes
Sautéed Spinach

Szechuan Pickled Vegetables

**8 servings
Preparation time:
15 minutes,
plus 2 to 5 days
pickling time**
1 pound (500g) cabbage
1 pound (500g) cucumber
4 ounces (100g) carrot
4 green bell peppers
1 stalk celery
3 dried red peppers, seeds removed and cut each into 2 to 3 pieces
For pickling:
3 tablespoons coarse salt
6 cups water
3 tablespoons rice wine

A typical Szechuan-style pickle dish.

Calories	35	Protein	1.8g	Fats	0.2g	Carbohydrates	5.6g

1. Bring 6 cups of water to a boil and add coarse salt, stirring until salt is dissolved. Allow the brine to cool to room temperature.
2. Cut cabbage and cucumber into bite-size pieces.
3. Peel carrot, core bell peppers, and remove any string from celery. Cut all of these into bite-size pieces.
4. Put vegetables and dried red peppers into a large pickling jar. Pour well-cooled brine over vegetables, covering completely. Pour rice wine in at the end.
5. Close the jar, making sure lid is tightly shut. Allow vegetables to pickle at room temperature. In the summertime, this pickling process should take from 2 to 3 days, but in the wintertime, it will take 4 to 5 days. When vegetables begin to have pungent and spicy flavor, store in the refrigerator.
6. Drain slightly when you serve.

Chilled Celery with Mustard

**4 servings
Cooking time:
10 minutes**
2 stalks celery
Dressing:
1 tablespoon sesame oil
1 tablespoon vinegar
½ tablespoon mustard
½ tablespoon sugar
1 teaspoon salt

Calories	38	Protein	0.4g	Fats	3.7g	Carbohydrates	2.6g

1. Remove strings from celery and cut celery into 2-inch (5cm) pencil-thick pieces.
2. Parboil celery until color begins to change. Remove quickly and rinse under cold running water until celery is cool. Drain well and chill in the refrigerator.
3. Combine ingredients for dressing and mix well.
4. Arrange celery in a dish, and pour dressing over it just before serving.

Eggplants with Soy Dressing

**4 servings
Cooking time:
25 minutes**
10 ounces (300g) thin eggplants
1 slice of ham, finely chopped
1 teaspoon finely chopped fresh ginger
1 teaspoon finely chopped parsley
Dressing:
1 clove of garlic, finely chopped
2 tablespoons soy sauce
1 tablespoon vinegar
1 teaspoon sesame oil
½ teaspoon salt
½ teaspoon sugar
½ teaspoon hot bean paste

A health-promoting recipe that works best with four to six small eggplants.

Calories	45	Protein	4.6g	Fats	1.8g	Carbohydrates	4.7g

1. Cut stems off eggplants. Place eggplants on a rack in a steamer and steam about 15 minutes or until soft. Let stand at room temperature until cool. Shred by hand into long strips and chill in the refrigerator.
2. Combine ingredients for dressing and mix well.
3. Arrange eggplants in a dish and sprinkle with ham, ginger, and parsley. Pour dressing over eggplants just before serving.

Sautéed Eggplants

Eggplant differs in size and shape from country to country. The original was supposedly an egg-shaped white one from which the name is derived.

Calories 179	Protein 5.0g	Fats 14.3g	Carbohydrates 7.1g

4 servings
Cooking time:
20 minutes

1 pound (500g) thin eggplants
1 green bell pepper
1 red bell pepper
2 ounces (50g) lean pork, thinly sliced
¼ teaspoon cornstarch
3 to 4 cups oil for deep-frying
1 tablespoon vegetable oil
1 tablespoon finely chopped spring onion
1 teaspoon finely chopped fresh ginger
1 clove of garlic, finely chopped
1 tablespoon rice wine
2 tablespoons soy sauce
½ teaspoon sugar

1. Cut stems off eggplants and cut into bite-size pieces. Soak for a few minutes in cold water. Drain well, and pat dry with paper towels to avoid splattering when you fry.
2. Cut green and red bell peppers into bite-size pieces.
3. Cut pork into bite-size pieces and coat with cornstarch.
4. Heat oil for deep-frying to 360°F (180°C) and deep-fry eggplants until brown. Drain well.
5. Heat 1 tablespoon of oil, and quickly stir-fry in spring onion, ginger, and garlic. Add pork and stir until color changes. Add bell peppers and then eggplants. Stir all ingredients well before adding rice wine, soy sauce, and sugar. Stir until well blended before serving.

Sautéed Tomatoes

These are a snap to make, requiring only that you use tomatoes fully ripened.

Calories 80	Protein 1.4g	Fats 5.1g	Carbohydrates 7.3g

4 servings
Cooking time:
10 minutes

4 ripe medium tomatoes
1½ tablespoons vegetable oil
1 tablespoon finely chopped spring onion
1 teaspoon salt
1 teaspoon sugar

1. Cut tomatoes into 8 wedges and discard seeds.
2. Heat oil and quickly stir-fry spring onion and tomatoes over high heat. Season with salt and sugar. Cook until juices are reduced to about half.

Sautéed Spinach

Spinach is a vegetable chock-full of vitamins, especially the vitamin A in the carotene. Spinach works extremely well with oil and thus has excellent digestive and absorptive qualities.

Calories 87	Protein 3.0g	Fats 6.7g	Carbohydrates 4.3g

4 servings
Cooking time:
10 minutes

¾ pound (350g) spinach
2 tablespoons vegetable oil
1 tablespoon finely chopped spring onion
1 clove of garlic, finely chopped
1 teaspoon salt
½ teaspoon sugar

1. Cut spinach into 3-inch (7.5 cm) long pieces.
2. Heat oil, add spring onion and garlic, and stir slightly before adding spinach. Stir-fry spinach quickly over high heat. Season with salt and sugar, and stir thoroughly before serving.

Chinese Home-Style Potatoes
Peas with Ground Beef

Stewed Acorn Squash
String Beans and Tomatoes

Chinese Home-Style Potatoes

4 servings
Cooking time:
25 minutes
2 large potatoes
4 ounces (100g) lean beef,
  thinly sliced
Seasoning for beef:
  ⅔ teaspoon rice wine
  ⅔ teaspoon soy sauce
  ⅔ teaspoon cornstarch
3 to 4 cups oil for deep-frying
1½ tablespoons vegetable oil
1 tablespoon coarsely chopped
  spring onion
1 teaspoon julienned
  fresh ginger
1 tablespoon rice wine
½ teaspoon salt
2 tablespoons soy sauce
½ teaspoon sugar

This is one of my own favorties. Although a little higher in calories than other vegetable dishes, nothing quite matches its taste and nutrition.

Calories 176	Protein 7.7g	Fats 8.8g	Carbohydrates 14.8g

1. Peel potatoes and cut into thin slices. Soak in cold water a few minutes (photo A). Drain potatoes and pat dry to prevent splattering when frying.
2. Cut beef into 1-inch (2.5cm) long strips. Sprinkle with rice wine and soy sauce, and mix lightly. Just before cooking, coat with cornstarch.
3. Heat oil for deep-frying to 360°F (180°C) and deep-fry potatoes until lightly golden. Remove them from oil and drain well (photo B).
4. Heat 1½ tablespoons of oil and stir-fry spring onion and ginger lightly. Add beef and stir-fry. When color of beef begins to change, add fried potatoes and season with rice wine, salt, soy sauce, and sugar. Stir until ingredients are thoroughly mixed (photo C).

A. Cut potatoes into thin slices and soak in cold water to prevent discoloring.

B. Pat potatoes dry and deep-fry until lightly golden.

C. Stir-fry spring onion, ginger, and beef. Add fried potatoes and season.

Peas with Ground Beef

4 servings
Cooking time:
15 minutes
½ pound (250g) frozen green
  peas
4 canned mushrooms
6 ounces (150g) lean ground beef
Seasoning for ground beef:
  2 teaspoons flour
  1 teaspoon rice wine
  1 teaspoon soy sauce
  Pinch of salt
  Twist of black pepper
1½ tablespoons vegetable oil
1 tablespoon coarsely chopped
  spring onion
1 teaspoon thinly sliced
  fresh ginger
1 tablespoon rice wine
1 teaspoon salt
Pinch of salt

This is an ideal dish when fresh green peas are in season, although frozen will of course do equally well. When using fresh peas, be sure to boil them in salted boiling water until green and just tender.

Calories 228	Protein 11.9g	Fats 13.8g	Carbohydrates 9.8g

1. Allow green peas to thaw to room temperature.
2. Cut each of mushrooms into 2 to 3 thin slices.
3. Combine ground beef with flour, rice wine, soy sauce, salt, and pepper and mix well.
4. Heat oil and stir-fry spring onion and ginger slightly. Add ground beef and stir until color of beef changes. Add mushrooms and green peas and stir well.
5. Season with rice wine, salt, and pepper and mix well. Add dissolved cornstarch and stir quickly until sauce thickens.

Twist of black pepper
½ teaspoon cornstarch dissolved
  in 1 teaspoon water

Stewed Acorn Squash

Another vegetarian dish rich in vitamin A. The combination of acorn squash lightly cooked in vegetable oil and then simmered in soy sauce creates a unique kind of flavor that will please everyone.

Calories 169	Protein 3.3g	Fats 4.7g	Carbohydrates 30.7g

6 servings
Cooking time:
30 minutes

2 pounds (1kg) acorn squash or Chinese pumpkin
2 tablespoons vegetable oil
2 tablespoons coarsely chopped spring onion
2 tablespoons soy sauce
½ tablespoon sugar
1 cup water

1. Cut acorn squash in half and scoop out and discard seeds. Cut squash into 1½-inch (4cm) squares.
2. Heat oil and stir-fry spring onion and squash.
3. Add soy sauce and sugar with water. Stir, put lid on, and simmer over low heat until squash is tender.

String Beans and Tomatoes

A low-calorie vegetarian dish that strikes a neat balance between the nutritious combination of vegetables and the slightly salty flavor.

Calories 85	Protein 1.9g	Fats 6.7g	Carbohydrates 4.5g

4 servings
Cooking time:
30 minutes

½ pound (250g) string beans
1 ripe tomato
2 tablespoons vegetable oil
¼ onion, peeled and coarsely chopped
1 teaspoon salt
Twist of pepper

1. Trim both ends of string beans and remove strings. Cut beans into halves.
2. Seed tomato and dice into cubes.
3. Heat oil, and quickly stir-fry beans until color changes. Remove from the wok and reserve.
4. Stir-fry onion quickly until soft, and add tomato, stirring until juice comes out.
5. Return beans to tomato. Season with salt and pepper. Lower heat, place cover on, and simmer until beans are tender.

Asparagus with Crabmeat

Here is another simple-to-make dish, since both the asparagus and the crabmeat come from cans. It is also low in calories and tasty as well.

Calories 61	Protein 4.0g	Fats 3.4g	Carbohydrates 2.7g

4 servings
Cooking time:
15 minutes

8 spears canned white asparagus
4 ounces (100g) canned crabmeat
1 tablespoon vegetable oil
1 cup chicken broth
1 tablespoon rice wine
½ teaspoon salt
Twist of black pepper
2 teaspoons cornstarch dissolved in 1½ tablespoons water

1. Empty the contents of the can of asparagus into a dish and steam 10 minutes.
2. Remove cartilage from crabmeat and crumble into flakes.
3. Heat oil and quickly sauté crabmeat. Add chicken broth, rice wine, salt, and pepper. Stir well and when ingredients come to a boil, add dissolved cornstarch and stir until sauce thickens.
4. Drain liquid from steamed asparagus and arrange on a plate. Pour crabmeat sauce over asparagus.

Asparagus with Crabmeat
Vegetables
with Chicken and Abalone

Green Vegetables with Dried Scallops

Vegetables with Chicken and Abalone

4 servings
Cooking time:
1 hour
30 minutes,
plus 6 to 8 hours
for soaking
dried scallops
2 dried scallops
10 ounces (300g) chicken
    pieces with bone
1-inch (2.5cm) piece of spring
    onion
1 thin slice of fresh ginger
6 to 7 cups water
1 pound (500g) Chinese cabbage
4 dried mushrooms
1 ounce (25g) canned bamboo
    shoots
1 piece of canned abalone
2 thin slices of ham
1 tablespoon rice wine
2 teaspoons salt
Pinch of sugar

A rich mix of wholesome vegetables. The calorie count is a little higher than other vegetable dishes because of the chicken, but the overall taste is hard to match.

Calories	198	Protein	25.7g	Fats	11.3g	Carbohydrates	5.5g

1. Soak dried scallops in hot water 6 to 8 hours until soft, then crumble into flakes by hand.

2. Place chicken pieces in a soup pot with spring onion, ginger, and water. Bring to a boil, skimming off as much foam as possible. Lower heat and simmer 1 hour.

3. Chop Chinese cabbage into bite-size pieces.

4. Soak dried mushrooms in warm water until soft and remove stems. Save the water the mushrooms were soaked in. Cut mushrooms diagonally into 2 to 3 pieces each.

5. Cut bamboo shoots into thin slices.

6. Slice abalone into thin pieces.

7. Slice ham into 6 to 8 pieces each.

8. Remove spring onion and ginger from chicken and discard. Add mushrooms and the water the mushrooms were soaked in, cabbage, and bamboo shoots. Simmer over low heat another 20 minutes.

9. Add abalone, scallops and ham. Season with rice wine, salt, and sugar and cook another 5 to 10 minutes before serving.

Green Vegetables with Dried Scallops

4 servings
Cooking time:
20 minutes,
plus 6 to 8 hours
for soaking
dried scallops
3 dried scallops
2 bunches of white stem sections
    of Chinese green cabbage or
    Chinese cabbage
8 dried mushrooms
2 ounces (50g) canned bamboo
    shoots
3 tablespoons vegetable oil
Pinch of salt
1½ cup chicken broth
2 ounces (50g) canned whole
    mushrooms, cut in half
½ teaspoon salt
2 teaspoons cornstarch dissolved
    with 1½ tablespoons water

Another healthful and savory vegetable dish. The photo on page 59 shows the Chinese green cabbage qing geng cai, but the stem sections of Chinese cabbage work equally well.

Calories	123	Protein	6.9g	Fats	10.2g	Carbohydrates	5.9g

1. Soak dried scallops in hot water 6 to 8 hours until soft, then crumble into flakes by hand.

2. Cut Chinese green cabbage lengthwise in half or quarters, depending on its size (see photo on page 59).

3. Soak dried mushrooms in warm water until soft, then remove stems. Cut mushrooms diagonally into 2 to 3 slices each.

4. Cut bamboo shoots into thin slices.

5. Heat 1½ tablespoons of oil and quickly stir-fry Chinese green cabbage with pinch of salt. Add half a cup of chicken broth. Cook over high heat 5 to 6 minutes, stirring occasionally until cabbage is tender. Remove cabbage and reserve.

6. Heat the remaining 1½ tablespoons of oil and quickly stir-fry mushrooms, scallops, bamboo shoots, and canned mushrooms. Add 1 cup of chicken broth and ½ teaspoon salt, then simmer 5 minutes.

7. Arrange cabbage, scallops, and vegetables on a plate. Be sure to save the liquid in the wok from frying scallops and vegetables.

8. Heat the liquid remaining in the wok. Add dissolved cornstarch and stir constantly until it thickens. Pour over vegetables and scallops.

EGG & BEANCURD DISHES

Eggs (chicken eggs) contain about 80 calories each, and are often referred to as the perfect food because of their overall nutritional balance. Some people avoid them on the basis of the cholesterol they contain, but such concern is hardly warranted when consumption is kept to just one or two eggs a day.

Beancurd (tofu), an end-product of processed soy beans, is a vegetable protein which in recent years has been attracting much attention as a low-fat, low-calorie food. In Chinese cooking, both eggs and beancurd are commonly used. The dishes presented in this section, however, have been selected with an eye to their suitability for health and fitness.

Egg Foo Yong

Mu Shu Pork

Steamed Custard with Clams

Baked Crabmeat Omelet

Egg Foo Yong

4 servings
Cooking time:
15 minutes
2 ounces (50g) canned or fresh
   crabmeat
½ tablespoon rice wine
1 dried mushroom
1 ounce (25g) canned bamboo
   shoots
6 eggs
1 teaspoon finely chopped
   spring onion
½ teaspoon salt
4 tablespoons vegetable oil
Garnish:
   Parsley

Foo Yong is actually the name of a flower in Chinese, one that is pretty, light and fluffy—just like this dish.

Calories 256	Protein 11.7g	Fats 21.6g	Carbohydrates 2.0g

1. Remove cartilage from crab-meat and crumble into flakes. Sprinkle crabmeat with rice wine.
2. Soak dried mushroom in warm water until soft, then remove stem. Cut mushroom into fine strips. Cut bamboo shoots also into fine strips.
3. Break eggs and beat slightly. Add mushroom, bamboo shoots, spring onion, and ⅔ of crabmeat along with salt (photo A).
4. Heat oil until very hot and begins to smoke. Pour egg mixture and cook until half done. Turn omelet over and cook the other side (photo B).
5. Scatter the remaining crabmeat on top of omelet and garnish with parsley before serving.

A. Beat eggs slightly with chopsticks or fork and add vegetables and ⅔ of crabmeat with salt.

B. Heat oil until it begins to smoke and pour egg mixture. Cook until half done and turn over.

Mu Shu Pork

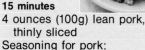

4 servings
Cooking time:
15 minutes
4 ounces (100g) lean pork,
   thinly sliced
Seasoning for pork:
   1 teaspoon rice wine
   1 tablespoon soy sauce
   1 teaspoon cornstarch
2 dried mushrooms
10 dried wood-ear mushrooms
2 ounces (50g) canned bamboo
   shoots
4 ounces (100g) spinach
4-inch (10cm) piece of spring
   onion
3 eggs
Pinch of salt
6 tablespoons vegetable oil
2 teaspoons finely julienned
   fresh ginger

A familiar stir-fry of eggs, meat, and vegetables.

Calories 315	Protein 12.0g	Fats 26.9g	Carbohydrates 5.9g

1. Cut pork into thin strips. Sprinkle pork with rice wine, soy sauce, and cornstarch and mix lightly.
2. Soak dried mushrooms in warm water until soft and remove stems. Cut each mushroom into fine strips. Soak wood-ear mushrooms in warm water until they expand to about 5 times.
3. Cut bamboo shoots into thin strips. Cut spinach into 2-inch (5cm) lengths.
4. Slice spring onion diago-

1 tablespoon rice wine
1 tablespoon soy sauce
½ teaspoon salt

nally into ¼-inch (0.5cm) pieces.
5. Break eggs into a bowl, adding pinch of salt and beat slightly. Heat 3 tablespoons of oil until it begins to smoke and add eggs. When eggs have absorbed oil, scramble lightly. Remove eggs and reserve.
6. Heat the remaining 3 tablespoons of oil. Stir-fry spring onion and ginger quickly and add pork. When pork is cooked, add mushrooms, bamboo shoots, spinach, and wood-ear mushrooms. Season with rice wine, soy sauce, and salt. Return scrambled eggs and stir again, mixing everything well.

Steamed Custard with Clams

Savory custard so smooth that it can easily be served in place of a soup. The low calorie count encourages its use as a diet dish.

Calories	83	Protein	7.4g	Fats	5.1g	Carbohydrates	1.0g

4 servings
Cooking time:
30 minutes

½ pound (250g) clams in shell
1⅔ cups water
3 eggs
1 tablespoon finely chopped
   spring onion
Pinch of salt
1 thin slice of ham, finely
   chopped

1. Wash clams and place in a pot with water. Cook until clams open. Remove. Strain remaining clam broth with cheese cloth and set aside.
2. Break eggs in a bowl and beat lightly. Add spring onion, clam broth, and salt, and mix well.
3. Pour egg mixture into 4 individual cups and add clams. You may also pour the entire amount into a casserole.
4. Preheat an oven to 360°F (180°C) and cook in a bain-marie to steam egg and clam mixture 20 minutes. You may also use a steamer. Sprinkle custard with chopped ham and turn off heat.
5. Place cups on small saucers when serving.
Note: This dish may also be refrigerated and served cold.

Baked Crabmeat Omelet

This oven-baked Chinese omelet can also be served cold as finger food. It's the oven-baking that produces the interestingly different texture.

Calories	212	Protein	13.2g	Fats	15.3g	Carbohydrates	5.5g

4 servings
Cooking time:
30 minutes

2 ounces (50g) canned
   crabmeat
3 dried mushrooms
1 ounce (25g) canned bamboo
   shoots
2 tablespoons vegetable oil
1 tablespoon rice wine
1½ teaspoons salt
2 teaspoons sugar
6 eggs
½ cup chicken broth
2 tablespoons frozen green
   peas
Garnish:
   Parsley

1. Remove cartilage from crabmeat and crumble into flakes.
2. Soak dried mushrooms in warm water until soft and remove stems. Cut into thin strips.
3. Cut bamboo shoots into fine strips.
4. Heat oil and stir-fry mushrooms and bamboo shoots. Add crabmeat and season with rice wine, salt, and sugar. Stir ingredients well. Remove and set aside.
5. Break eggs into a bowl and beat lightly. Add chicken broth and crabmeat mixture and mix well.
6. Preheat an oven to 360°F (180°C). Pour egg and crabmeat mixture into a greased casserole or baking dish. Sprinkle with green peas and bake 20 minutes.
7. Remove omelet from the casserole and cut into bite-size pieces. Garnish with parsley before serving.

Spicy Beancurd Salad

Chilled Beancurd Salad

Beancurd with Crabmeat

Beancurd with Oyster Sauce

Spicy Beancurd Salad

Calories 110	Protein 8.3g	Fats 7.4g	Carbohydrates 3.1g

4 servings
Preparation time:
10 minutes
1 square beancurd (tofu)
1 dried mushroom
½ hard-boiled egg
1 thin slice of ham
1 ounce (25g) canned bamboo
  shoots
Dressing:
  1 tablespoon ground sesame
    seeds
  2 tablespoons soy sauce
  ½ teaspoon sugar
  1 teaspoon sesame oil
Garnish:
  Cilantro

1. Rinse beancurd with cold water and drain thoroughly. Place in the refrigerator to chill.
2. Soak dried mushroom in warm water until soft, then remove stem.
3. Chop mushroom, hard-boiled egg, ham, and bamboo shoots for salad topping.
4. Combine all ingredients for dressing and mix well.
5. Cut beancurd into bite-size pieces and arrange on a plate. Sprinkle beancurd with salad topping. Add dressing and garnish with cilantro just before serving.

Chilled Beancurd Salad

4 servings
Preparation time:
10 minutes
1 square beancurd (tofu)
1 thin slice of ham, finely chopped
1 tablespoon Chinese salted
  pickles of cucumber or dilled
  pickles of cucumber, finely
  chopped
1 tablespoon finely chopped
  spring onion
1 teaspoon finely chopped
  fresh ginger
1 teaspoon finely chopped garlic
Dressing:
  2 tablespoons soy sauce
  1 teaspoon sesame oil
  ½ teaspoon hot bean paste
  Pinch of salt

A salad that is quick and easy yet doesn't skimp on taste or nutrition. Makes an ideal chilled summer dish.

Calories 91	Protein 6.9g	Fats 5.5g	Carbohydrates 3.2g

1. Rinse beancurd with cold water and drain thoroughly. Place in the refrigerator to chill.
2. Combine all ingredients for dressing and mix well.
3. Cut beancurd into bite-size pieces and arrange on a plate. Sprinkle beancurd with finely chopped ham, pickles, spring onion, ginger, and garlic and pour dressing on just before serving.

Beancurd with Crabmeat

4 servings
Cooking time:
10 minutes
1 square beancurd (tofu)
4 ounces (100g) canned crabmeat
Season for crabmeat:
  1 teaspoon rice wine
  ½ teaspoon fresh ginger juice
3 tablespoons vegetable oil
1 tablespoon finely chopped
  spring onion
1 teaspoon finely julienned
  fresh ginger
2 tablespoons frozen green
  peas, slightly thawed
½ teaspoon sugar
1 teaspoon salt
1 teaspoon cornstarch dissolved
  in 2 teaspoons water

The delicate texture of beancurd in a dish that is easier and quicker to make than Beancurd Salad.

Calories 182	Protein 10.1g	Fats 13.9g	Carbohydrates 2.6g

1. Cut beancurd into 1-inch (2.5cm) cubes. Place beancurd in a strainer and pour boiling water over it. Drain well.
2. Remove cartilage from crabmeat and crumble into flakes. Sprinkle with rice wine and ginger juice.
3. Heat oil and stir-fry spring onion and ginger lightly. Add crabmeat, beancurd, and peas, and stir again. Season with sugar and salt.
4. When all ingredients begin to simmer, add dissolved cornstarch, and quickly stir until sauce thickens.

Beancurd with Oyster Sauce

A beancurd dish with a taste that is truly delightful. Serve with plain rice, and add stir-fried vegetables or a salad for a well-rounded nutritious meal.

Calories 130g	Protein 6.4g	Fats 8.1g	Carbohydrates 7.8g

**4 servings
Cooking time:
15 minutes**

1 square beancurd (tofu)
1 tablespoon salt
1 tablespoon vegetable oil
½ cup chicken broth
2 tablespoons oyster sauce
1 teaspoon sugar
Twist of pepper
2 ounces (50g) sliced canned mushrooms
1 teaspoon cornstarch dissolved in 2 teaspoons water
2 tablespoons frozen green peas, slightly thawed
1 teaspoon sesame oil

1. Place beancurd in a bowl with salt and just enough water to cover. Let it stand 20 minutes. When removing beancurd, cut it lengthwise in half and then into 2-inch (5cm) squares about ½-inch (1cm) thick. Pat beancurd dry with a towel (photo A).
2. Heat oil and sauté beancurd until lightly golden on both sides (photo B). Arrange on a plate.
3. Combine chicken broth, oyster sauce, sugar, pepper, and mushrooms, and bring to a boil. Add dissolved cornstarch and stir. When sauce thickens, add peas and sesame oil.
4. Pour sauce over beancurd.

A. Cut beancurd into 2-inch (5cm) squares about ½- inch (1cm) thick and pat dry.
B. Heat oil in frying pan and sauté beancurd until lightly golden on both sides.

Beancurd and Fish Soup (see photo on page 70)

This is a good one-pot dish for cold winter nights. The hearty soup is calorie low and protein high. Use a bland white-fleshed fish for best results.

Calories 184	Protein 16.9g	Fats 10.6g	Carbohydrates 4.8g

**4 servings
Cooking time:
30 minutes**

1 square beancurd (tofu)
½ pound (250g) whitefisn (cod, sea bass or flounder)
3 tablespoons rice wine
3 dried mushrooms
2 ounces (50g) canned bamboo shoots
2 dried red peppers
2 tablespoons vegetable oil
2-inch (5cm) piece of spring onion, cut into 2 to 3 pieces
2 to 3 slices of fresh ginger
1 clove of garlic, thinly sliced
3 cups water
2 tablespoons soy sauce
1 teaspoon salt

1. Cut beancurd into 1½-inch (4cm) cubes.
2. Cut fish into similar size cubes and sprinkle with 1 tablespoon rice wine.
3. Soak dried mushrooms in warm water until soft and remove stems. Cut each mushroom diagonally into 2 to 3 pieces. Julienne bamboo shoots.
4. Remove stems and seeds from dried red peppers.
5. Heat oil and stir-fry spring onion, ginger, garlic, and dried red peppers briefly. Add fish and stir briskly until fish begins to brown.
6. Add water, mushrooms, and bamboo shoots. Season with 2 tablespoons rice wine, soy sauce, and salt. Bring to a boil and skim off foam and lower heat to a simmer. Add beancurd and simmer another 10 minutes.

Beancurd and Fish Soup
Beancurd with Ground Pork

Beancurd and Meatball Soup

Beancurd with Ground Pork

4 servings
Cooking time:
10 minutes
1 square beancurd (tofu)
2 dried mushrooms
2 dried wood-ear mushrooms
2 ounces (50g) canned bamboo
  shoots
3 tablespoons vegetable oil
1 tablespoon finely chopped
  spring onion
1 teaspoon finely chopped
  fresh ginger
2 ounces (50g) lean ground
  pork
2 tablespoons soy sauce
Pinch of sugar
½ teaspoon salt
1 teaspoon cornstarch dissolved
  in 2 teaspoons water

Preparations are easy. Lean pork is suggested for the ground meat if low fat is uppermost in your mind.

Calories	186	Protein	9.2g	Fats	15.1g	Carbohydrates	4.6g

1. Dice beancurd into small cubes.
2. Soak dried mushrooms in warm water until soft and remove stems. Cut into thin strips.
3. Soak dried wood-ear mushrooms in warm water until they expand to about 5 times. Drain well and wring gently. Cut into 2 or 3 pieces.
4. Julienne bamboo shoots.
5. Heat oil and stir-fry spring onion and ginger briefly and add following ingredients in order; ground pork, mushrooms, bamboo shoots and wood-ear mushrooms. Add beancurd and season with soy sauce, sugar, and salt. When mixture comes to a boil, add dissolved cornstarch and stir constantly until sauce thickens.
6. Pour this into large saucer and sprinkle with chopped shallots.

Garnish:
  Shallots, finely chopped

Beancurd and Meatball Soup

4 servings
Cooking time:
30 minutes
1 square beancurd (tofu)
10 ounces (300g) Chinese
  green cabbage or Chinese
  cabbage
4 dried mushrooms
1 ounce (25g) canned bamboo
  shoots
1 ounce(25g)bean thread noodles
1 ounce (25g) canned abalone
4 ounces (100g) ground pork
1 teaspoon finely chopped
  spring onion
Seasoning for ground pork:
  1 tablespoon rice wine
  ¼ teaspoon fresh ginger juice
  ½ teaspoon salt
  3 to 5 tablespoons water
  ½ tablespoon cornstarch
6 cups water
1½ teaspoons salt
Twist of black pepper

The light texture of the meatballs gives an added flavor to the broth. This soup is almost oil free and goes well with most vegetable dishes.

Calories	171	Protein	13.1g	Fats	9.0g	Carbohydrates	11.7g

1. Cut beancurd into 1-inch (2.5cm) cubes.
2. Cut Chinese green cabbage into large pieces.
3. Soak dried mushrooms in warm water until soft, then remove stems. Cut each mushroom diagonally into 2 to 3 pieces.
4. Cut bamboo shoots into thin slices.
5. Soak bean thread noodles in warm water until soft. Drain well and wring out excess water.
6. Slice abalone into thin pieces.
7. Combine ground pork, spring onion, rice wine, ginger juice, and salt in a bowl and mix well. Gradually add from 3 to 5 tablespoons of water and cornstarch to form sticky consistency. Wet your hands with water and use 1 tablespoon of meat mixture and roll into ball. Repeat this.
8. Bring water to a boil and gently add meatballs. Skim off as much foam as possible. When meatballs float to the surface, remove. Add mushrooms, bamboo shoots, abalone, and Chinese green cabbage and bring to a boil. Lower heat and cook until vegetables are soft. Add salt and pepper to taste. Add bean thread noodles and meatballs and bring to a boil again.

●**Beancurd and Fish Soup . . . See page 69**

RICE DISHES & PASTA

There is much speculation on whether rice or flour is better for health and fitness. It is difficult to come down on the side of one as opposed to the other, since both are important calorie-sources from carbohydrates and are alike in that they need to be taken in conjunction with other foods containing other essential proteins and vitamins.

Both rice and pasta dishes are well represented in Chinese cooking, but the sampling introduced in the following pages consists chiefly of ones that, being easy to cook, are popular. Their suitability as dishes for health and fitness has also been taken into consideration.

Fried Rice with Spinach
Fried Rice with Crabmeat and Lettuce

Beef and Vegetable Rice
Curried Lamb and Rice

Fried Rice with Spinach

4 servings
Cooking time:
10 minutes,
plus cooking
time of rice

3 cups cooked rice (see below
for How to Cook Rice)
4 ounces (100g) spinach
3 tablespoons vegetable oil
2 tablespoons finely chopped
spring onion
3 ounces (80g) chopped canned
mushrooms
Pinch of salt
Twist of black pepper

Fried rice is a well-known Chinese dish and simply plain rice lightly stir-fried with other ingredients. Vitamin-rich spinach adds to its healthfulness.

Calories 231	Protein 3.9g	Fats 10.3g	Carbohydrates 30.4g

1. Cook rice in advance.
2. Blanch spinach in salted water. Remove spinach and rinse with cold water and wring dry completely. Chop into fine pieces.
3. Heat oil and stir-fry spring onion briefly. Add loosened rice and stir again until thoroughly mixed.
4. Add spinach and mushrooms and stir thoroughly. Add salt and pepper to taste.

Fried Rice with Crabmeat and Lettuce

4 servings
Cooking time:
10 minutes,
plus cooking
time of rice

3 cups cooked rice (see below
for How to Cook Rice)
2 large leaves lettuce
1 thin slice of ham
4 ounces (100g) canned crabmeat
1½ tablespoons vegetable oil
2 eggs, beaten lightly
1 teaspoon salt
½ teaspoon soy sauce
3 tablespoons chicken broth
2 tablespoons coarsely chopped
spring onion

So colorful and pretty that it's a delight to the eye as well as the appetite—which makes over-eating easy to do, so calorie-counters take notice!

Calories 257	Protein 11.2g	Fats 9.2g	Carbohydrates 29.7g

1. Cook rice in advance.
2. Julienne lettuce and chop ham coarsely.
3. Remove cartilage from crabmeat and crumble into flakes.
4. Heat 1 tablespoon of oil and scramble eggs quickly.
5. Add loosened rice into scrambled eggs. Add remaining ½ tablespoon of oil and stir quickly. Add rest of ingredients in following order: crabmeat, lettuce, salt, soy sauce, chicken broth and spring onion. Stir everything thoroughly.
6. Place fried rice on a plate and sprinkle with ham before serving.

How to Cook Rice

Chinese food has traditionally been served with plain rice, but can also be eaten with fried rice. Fried rice is plain rice which has been stir-fried with any variety of ingredients.

Directions:
1. Rinse rice, gently stirring with your hands, until water is almost clear when you pour it out.
2. Cook rice in a deep pot with heavy bottom and tight-fitting lid if you do not have a rice cooker. Put rice in the pot and add water the amount same as rice. Let rice soak 30 minutes.
3. Cook over medium heat 4 to 5 minutes. Then turn heat to high and bring to a boil. Reduce heat to low and cook 5 to 10 minutes. Turn off heat and let stand 10 to 15 minutes with lid on. You may loosen rice with a wet wooden spatula, and place dry towel under lid to absorb excess moisture.

Beef and Vegetable Rice

The salt and the rice wine are mainly responsible for giving this rice dish a lighter flavor than that found in Curried Lamb and Rice below.

Calories	420	Protein	19.6g	Fats	14.3g	Carbohydrates	49.5g

**4 servings
Cooking time:
40 minutes**

1. Rinse rice and let soak in cold water 10 minutes. Drain well.
2. Cut beef into ½-inch (1cm) pieces. Sprinkle with salt and pepper and mix slightly.
3. Chop onion and carrot coarsely.
4. In a stewing pot, heat 2 tablespoons of oil and sauté onion and carrot until color changes. Add beef and sauté until color of beef changes. Add mushrooms.

5. Add rice, chicken broth, rice wine, and salt to beef and vegetables and bring to a boil. Mix rice well by stirring thoroughly. Put lid on and lower heat. Simmer over very low heat 15 minutes or until rice is nearly done.
6. When rice is cooked, add peas and mix well. Turn off heat and let stand with lid closed 10 minutes before serving.

1½ cups uncooked rice
½ pound (250g) lean beef, thinly sliced
Seasoning for beef:
  Pinch of salt
  Twist of black pepper
½ onion
2 ounces (50g) carrot
3 tablespoons vegetable oil
3 ounces (80g) sliced canned mushrooms
1½ cups chicken broth or water
1 tablespoon rice wine
2 teaspoons salt
2 tablespoons frozen green peas, thawed

Curried Lamb and Rice

What might be called a Chinese-style pilaf. The highly compatible flavors of curry, lamb, vegetables and raisins combine with the nutritional element to make this a truly excellent rice dish.

Calories	598	Protein	29.7g	Fats	25.6g	Carbohydrates	57.9g

**4 servings
Cooking time:
40 minutes**

1. Rinse rice and let soak in cold water 10 minutes. Drain well.
2. Cut lamb into ½-inch (1cm) cubes.
3. Remove strings from celery and chop coarsely.
4. In a stewing pot, heat oil and sauté onion until color changes. Add lamb and sauté until color changes.
5. Add celery, rice, curry pow-

der and chicken broth and bring to a boil. Mix rice well by stirring thoroughly. Put lid on a pot and lower heat. Simmer over very low heat 15 minutes or until rice is nearly done.
6. When rice is cooked, add ginger juice, salt, pepper, and raisins and mix well. Turn off heat and let stand with lid closed 10 minutes before serving.

1½ cups uncooked rice
1 pound (500g) boneless lamb
1 stalk of celery
2 tablespoons vegetable oil
1 onion, chopped
2 teaspoons curry powder
1½ cups chicken broth or water
2 teaspoons fresh ginger juice
1 teaspoon salt
Twist of black pepper
3 tablespoons raisins, soaked 5 minutes in water to cover

Poached Chinese Dumplings

Chinese Pan-Fried Meat Pie

Poached Chinese Dumplings

**Makes
50 dumplings
Cooking time:
1 hour
30 minutes**

Dough for wrappers:
   2 cups sifted all-purpose flour
   ½ cup warm water, plus 1 to
   2 tablespoons
Meat filling:
   ½ pound (250g) ground pork
   1 pound (500g) Chinese
    cabbage
   2 tablespoons finely chopped
    spring onion
   ¼ teaspoon fresh ginger juice
   1½ teaspoons salt
   1 tablespoon rice wine
   2 tablespoons soy sauce
   1 tablespoon sesame oil
Condiments for dumplings:
   Soy sauce, vinegar, hot bean
   paste

One of the popular classics of Chinese cooking. Like the Italian ravioli with which it is often compared, it is a dough-wrapper stuffed with meat and vegetables. In addition to the serving idea introduced here, the dumplings can also be boiled to be served in soups, and are even versatile enough to be pan-fried or steamed.

Calories 32	Protein 1.4g	Fats 1.3g	Carbohydrates 3.3g

(1 piece)

Making wrappers
1. Place flour in a bowl and add warm water gradually, mixing well (photo A). Knead dough until soft, but not sticky, on a lightly floured board. Shape dough into ball and cover with damp cloth. Let dough sit 30 minutes (photos B, C).

2. Knead dough, and roll into long cylinder 1-inch (2.5cm) in diameter. Cut into 50 even pieces (photo D).

3. Flatten each piece of dough with palm of your hand and use a rolling pin to roll into thin 2½-inch (6cm) circles in diameter (photo E). Leave center of wrapper thicker than edges as you roll to keep wrapper from breaking.

Making filling
1. Blanch Chinese cabbage until soft and drain well. Chop into very fine pieces and squeeze out as much liquid as possible.

A. Add warm water gradually to flour, mixing well.

B. Knead dough until smooth and soft.

C. Cover dough with damp cloth and let it sit 30 minutes.

D. Roll dough into long cylinder 1-inch (2.5cm) in diameter. Cut into 50 pieces.

E. Roll each piece into thin circles 2½-inch (6cm) in diameter.

F. Place about 1 tablespoon of filling on the center of wrapper.

G. Fold in half forming a crescent shape.

H. Pinch edges with thumb and forefinger making creases on one edge.

I. Close the seam firmly so that it will not open.

2. Combine ground pork, spring onion and ginger juice in a bowl and add other seasonings. Mix well. Add Chinese cabbage and mix again.

Forming dumplings

1. Place about 1 tablespoon of filling on each wrapper and fold in half, forming a crescent shape (photos F, G). Close the seam firmly (photos H, I). Repeat to make 50 dumplings.

2. Fill a soup pot about ¾ full with water and bring to a boil. Put dumplings in one by one. When water comes to a second boil, add 1 cup of cold water and lower heat a little. When water comes to third boil and dumplings float up and become translucent with meat sticking to wrapper, remove dumplings with a slotted spoon. Place dumplings on a large plate, or in individual portions on small plates, and sprinkle with a little bit of water they were cooked in to keep from sticking together.

Serving

Provide each person with small saucer to mix soy sauce and vinegar in. Dip each dumpling into this sauce as you eat them. You may also add hot bean paste to sauce if you like.

Chinese Pan-Fried Meat Pie

This is similar in taste to the well-known Chinese dumplings called "Pot Stickers," although a little more work is required here because of the need to make the ruffled edges.

Calories 67	Protein 3.0g	Fats 2.8g	Carbohydrates 6.8g

(1 piece)

Makes
25 pieces
Cooking time:
1 hour
30 minutes

1. Prepare 50 of wrappers as in Poached Chinese Dumplings.

2. Blanch cabbage and celery until color begins to change. Remove and rinse with cold running water. Drain well and chop into fine pieces, squeezing out any excess liquid.

3. Combine ground beef, cabbage, celery, spring onion, ginger juice, soy sauce, rice wine, salt, and sesame oil and mix well. Divide into 25 equal parts.

4. Take 25 of wrappers and place in center of each one a portion of filling, leaving outer edge of wrapper dry. Place another wrapper on top and gently pinch edges of top and bottom together with your thumb and index finger. Hold pie flat in your left hand and with your right thumb, fold over ½-inch (1cm) of edge toward center and repeat this around edge (photos A, B).

5. Heat oil in a frying pan and fry each side until surface is golden brown and slightly puffed out, and begins to bubble. Turn pies over several times to ensure even cooking to center, making sure color is even (photo C).

6. Serve with soy sauce and vinegar as you would with Poached Chinese Dumplings. You may also serve them plain.

Dough for wrappers:
2 cups sifted all-purpose flour
¾ cup hot water, plus 1 to 2 tablespoons

Meat filling:
½ pound (250g) lean ground beef
½ pound (250g) cabbage
2 stalks celery, strings removed
1 tablespoon finely chopped spring onion
½ teaspoon fresh ginger juice
½ tablespoon soy sauce
1 tablespoon rice wine
1 teaspoon salt
2 tablespoons sesame oil
2 tablespoons vegetable oil

Condiments:
Soy sauce, vinegar

A. Place wrapper on top of one with filling and seal edges tightly.

B. Fold edge slightly over with thumb and forefinger and press toward center.

C. Heat oil in a frying pan and fry until golden brown on both sides.

Chinese Steamed Buns

Siu Mai

Fried Noodles with Vegetables

Fried Noodles with Beef

Chinese Steamed Buns

Makes 20 buns
Cooking time:
3 hours
Dough for buns:
  4 cups sifted all-purpose flour
  1 teaspoon active dry yeast
  1 cup warm water, about 110°F
    (45°C)
  1 tablespoon sugar
  ½ teaspoon salt
Meat filling for 10 buns:
  4 ounces (100g) ground pork
  ½ pound (250g) Chinese
    cabbage
  ½ tablespoon finely chopped
    spring onion
  ½ teaspoon fresh ginger juice
  1 tablespoon sesame oil
  2 teaspoons soy sauce
  ½ teaspoon salt
Spinach filling for 10 buns:
  ½ pound (250g) spinach
  ½ tablespoon sesame oil
  1 teaspoon salt

Calories	101	Protein	3.8g	Fats	2.9g	Carbohydrates	16.3g

(1 meat bun)

Calories	88	Protein	2.4g	Fats	1.0g	Carbohydrates	16.5g

(1 spinach bun)

Making dough

1. Place flour into a bowl. Dissolve yeast in warm water and add sugar and salt. When mixture begins to bubble, pour into flour. Mix well. Knead dough on a lightly floured board until soft. Place dough in the bowl and cover with a damp cloth and allow to rinse about 1½ hours at about 85°F (30°C).

2. When dough has risen to double its original size, punch down and knead well. Form dough into long cylinder 2-inch (5cm) in diameter and cut into 20 even pieces. Allow to rise for a few minutes.

3. Flatten each piece with palms of your hands and roll into 5-inch (12cm) rounds. Leave center of wrapper thicker than edges to ensure well-formed bun that steams correctly.

Making filling

1. Meat filling is the same as filling for Poached Chinese Dumplings on page 80.

2. Spinach filling is made by parboiling spinach in salted water. When color begins to change, remove spinach, drain, and wring thoroughly dry. Chop into fine pieces and squeeze out any excess liquid. Add sesame oil and salt and mix well.

Forming Buns

1. Place filling in center of dough. Cup this in your left hand and fold edges up toward center. Twist shut.

2. Allow buns to rise another 10 minutes. Place layer of moist cheesecloth on bottom of a steamer and place buns on it. Remember to leave some space between buns as they expand. Steam at high heat 20 minutes.

Siu Mai

Makes
20 pieces
Cooking time:
1 hour
30 minutes
Dough for wrappers:
  1 cup sifted all-purpose flour
  ¼ cup water, plus 1 to 2
    teaspoons
Filling:
  2 medium shrimps
  ½ pound (250g) ground pork
  1 teaspoon rice wine
  ½ teaspoon salt
  1 teaspoon sesame oil
  ½ tablespoon soy sauce
  1 teaspoon sugar
1 scrambled egg
1 thin slice of ham, finely chopped
1 green bell pepper, quickly
  parboiled and finely chopped
Condiments for Siu Mai:
  Soy sauce, vinegar, mustard,
  hot bean paste

Calories	54	Protein	3.7g	Fats	2.2g	Carbohydrates	4.1g

(1 piece)

Making wrappers

1. Place flour in a bowl and gradually add water. Mix well and knead dough until slightly firm. Cover dough with a damp cloth and let it stand 30 minutes.

2. Sprinkle pastry board lightly with cornstarch. Knead dough into a long cylinder 1-inch (2.5cm) in diameter. Cut into 20 pieces. Roll out as in Poached Chinese Dumpling on page 80.

3. Take 4 to 5 wrappers and sprinkle each one lightly with cornstarch and stack them up on top of each other. Use a rolling pin and roll them out and frill the edges of wrappers slightly.

Making filling

Shell and devein shrimps. Chop into fine pieces and mix with ground pork. Add seasonings and mix well.

Forming Siu Mai

1. Spoon about 1 tablespoon filling in the center of wrapper and squeeze wrapper and filling to form Siu Mai. Garnish with a little egg, ham, and green bell pepper.

2. Line a steamer with a wet cheese-cloth and arrange Siu Mai, making sure edges do not touch. Steam over high heat 10 minutes.

3. Serve with small saucers with soy sauce and vinegar. You may also use mustard or hot bean paste.

Fried Noodles with Vegetables

| Calories 335 | Protein 13.8g | Fats 15.7g | Carbohydrates 32.8g |

**4 servings
Cooking time:
20 minutes**

6 ounces (150g) uncooked
  Chinese noodles
½ teaspoon sesame oil
6 ounces (150g) boneless
  chicken breast
Seasoning for chicken:
  1 teaspoon rice wine
  1 teaspoon soy sauce
  ½ teaspoon fresh ginger
    juice
  1 teaspoon cornstarch
2 dried mushrooms
1 ounce (25g) carrot
¼ stalk of celery
2 ounces (50g) canned bamboo
  shoots
4 snow peas
3 tablespoons vegetable oil
2 tablespoons finely chopped
  spring onion

1. Cook noodles in a pot of boiling water. When water reaches a second boil, add 1 cup of cold water and cook 10 minutes or until done. Strain noodles and rinse with cold water. Drain thoroughly. Add sesame oil and mix well.
2. Slice chicken into thin strips. Season with rice wine, soy sauce, and ginger juice. Sprinkle with cornstarch and mix well.
3. Soak dried mushrooms in warm water until soft and remove stems. Cut into thin strips.
4. Julienne carrot, celery, bamboo shoots, and snow peas.
5. Heat 1 tablespoon of oil and add and stir slightly vegetables in the following order: mushrooms, carrot, celery, bamboo shoots, and snow peas. Remove to a dish and reserve.
6. Heat 2 tablespoons of oil and stir-fry spring onion and ginger briefly and stir in chicken. When color of chicken changes, return vegetables to chicken, and stir again.
7. Season with rice wine, soy sauce, and sugar, and add cooked noodles, stirring everything thoroughly.

1 teaspoon finely julienned
  fresh ginger
1 tablespoon rice wine
2 tablespoons soy sauce
1 teaspoon sugar

Fried Noodles with Beef

China has numerous noodle dishes. Fried noodles, though a bit high in calories, are not only a delicious part of Chinese cooking in general but are just about indispensable.

| Calories 340 | Protein 12.9g | Fats 15.8g | Carbohydrates 35.1g |

**4 servings
Cooking time:
30 minutes**

6 ounces (150g) uncooked
  Chinese noodles
½ teaspoon sesame oil
4 ounces (100g) lean beef,
  thinly sliced
Seasoning for beef:
  1 teaspoon rice wine
  1 teaspoon soy sauce
  1 teaspoon cornstarch
4 ounces (100g) spinach
2 dried mushrooms
2 ounces (50g) canned bamboo
  shoots
4 tablespoons vegetable oil
2 tablespoons finely chopped
  spring onion
1½ cups chicken broth
1 tablespoon rice wine
1 tablespoon soy sauce
1 teaspoon sugar
1 teaspoon salt
Twist of black pepper
1½ tablespoons cornstarch dissolved in 3 tablespoons water

1. Prepare noodles as in Fried Noodles with Vegetables above.
2. Cut beef into bite-size pieces. Season with rice wine and soy sauce. Sprinkle with cornstarch and mix lightly.
3. Cut spinach into 2-inch (5cm) lengths.
4. Soak dried mushrooms in warm water until soft and remove stems. Slice each diagonally into 2 to 3 pieces.
5. Cut bamboo shoots into thin slices.
6. Heat 1 tablespoon of oil and add and stir slightly vegetables in the following order: mushrooms, bamboo shoots, and spinach. Remove to a dish and reserve.
7. Heat 1 tablespoon of oil and stir-fry spring onion briefly. Add beef and stir again quickly. When color of beef changes, return vegetables to beef, and stir again.
8. Add chicken broth, rice wine, soy sauce, sugar, salt, and pepper. When it comes to a boil, add dissolved cornstarch and stir constantly until sauce thickens.
9. Heat the remaining 2 tablespoons of oil in a frying pan. Spread out cooked noodles in the pan and fry on both sides until golden brown and crisp on the outside. Place noodles on a plate.
10. Pour meat sauce over noodles while still hot.

Mandarin Pancakes

Mandarin Pancakes

**Makes
20 pancakes
Cooking time:
1 hour
30 minutes**

Dough for pancakes:
2½ cups sifted all-purpose
  flour
¾ cup hot water
1 teaspoon sesame oil
Fillings:
Spinach and Bean Thread Noodles
1 pound (500g) spinach
2 ounces (50g) bean thread
  noodles
2 tablespoons vegetable oil
5 tablespoons chicken broth
2 tablespoons soy sauce
Shrimp and Scrambled Eggs
4 ounces (100g) shrimp
Seasoning for shrimp:
  ½ teaspoon rice wine
  ½ teaspoon fresh ginger juice
  1 teaspoon cornstarch
4 tablespoons vegetable oil
4 eggs
1 teaspoon salt
Bean Sprouts and Shallots
½ pound (250g) bean sprouts
4 ounces (100g) shallots
4 ounces (100g) lean pork,
  thinly sliced
Seasoning for pork:
  1 teaspoon rice wine
  1 teaspoon soy sauce
  ½ teaspoon cornstarch
4 tablespoons vegetable oil
1 tablespoon rice wine
1 tablespoon soy sauce
½ teaspoon salt
**Soy Sauce Pork (see Soy Sauce
Beef on page 13)**
Garnish and condiments:
  Spring onion, finely julienned
  Parsley
  Cilantro
  Black bean paste
  Chopped peanuts

Calories 206	Protein 11.0g	Fats 10.6g	Carbohydrates 14.8g

(1 pancake)

Making pancakes

1. Place flour in a bowl and gradually add hot water. Knead dough well until soft but not sticky. Cover dough with a damp cloth and let it stand 20 minutes.
2. Knead dough on a lightly floured board and make a long cylinder about 1-inch (2.5cm) in diameter. Cut cylinder into 20 pieces. Flatten each section lightly with palms of hands and roll into 3-inch (7.5cm) circles.
3. Take circles and brush each on one surface with sesame oil. Place two oiled sides together and carefully roll them to about 7-inch (18cm) in diameter (photo A). Pancakes should be very thin.
4. Fry pancakes into a lightly oiled frying pan over low heat. Turn once when the surface begins to bubble (photo B). Remove and peel two pancakes apart while still hot (photo C). Fold into half and serve covered with a cloth so they do not get cold.

Making fillings

Spinach and Bean Thread Noodles:
1. Cut spinach into 2-inch (5cm) lengths.
2. Soak bean thread noodles in warm water until soft. Drain and wring out excess water and cut into bite-size pieces.
3. Heat oil and stir-fry spinach briefly. Add bean thread noodles, chicken broth, and soy sauce. Mix well.

Shrimp and Scrambled Eggs:
1. Shell and devein shrimp and add seasoning, mixing well.
2. Heat 1 tablespoon of oil and stir-fry shrimp until color changes and remove.
3. Beat eggs briefly and add salt. Add shrimp to eggs.
4. Heat the remaining 3 tablespoons of oil until it begins to smoke. Pour eggs in and scramble quickly.

Bean Sprouts and Shallots:
1. Trim off ends of bean sprouts. Cut shallots into 2-inch (5cm) lengths.
2. Slice pork into thin strips and add seasonings, mixing well.
3. Heat 2 tablespoons of oil and stir-fry bean sprouts briefly. Remove and reserve.
4. Heat the remaining 2 tablespoons of oil and stir-fry pork until color changes and add shallots, stirring over high heat. Add seasoning and return bean sprouts, stirring well.

Soy Sauce Pork:
Prepare pork (boneless loin roast) as in Soy Sauce Beef on page 13, substituting beef with pork. When pork has been cooked 1 hour, slice it into thin slices and garnish with parsley.

Serving

Arrange pancakes, fillings, and condiments on a large plate. Have each person take a pancake and put a combination of various fillings on it. Fold over or wrap in a roll and eat with your hands.

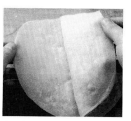

A. Roll 2 pancakes brushed with oil into circles 7-inch (18cm) in diameter.

B. Lightly fry on both sides until small bubbles form on the surface.

C. While pancake is still hot, peel 2 apart. Keep hot until you are ready to serve.

SOUPS

In Chinese cooking, soups are the foods with the lowest calories, although of course that will vary according to what goes into them. Unlike the western custom of having soups come at the start of the meal, in China they are usually served at the conclusion and thus signal that the meal is ending.

The deciding factor in what makes a soup good or bad is the stock. The clear chicken broth available at stores can of course be used; but from the standpoint of taste, home-made soups are best. In the section that follows I have mainly presented soups based on chicken stock and soups made by simmering meats and vegetables.

Chicken and Corn Soup
Egg Drop Soup with Tomatoes
Four Treasures Soup

Chicken and Vegetable Soup
Beancurd and
Mushroom Soup

Chicken and Corn Soup

4 servings
Cooking time:
20 minutes
2 ounces (50g) boneless chicken
  breast
3 tablespoons water
1 teaspoon rice wine
¼ teaspoon fresh ginger juice
1 cup sweet cream-style corn
2 cups chicken broth
1 teaspoon salt
1 tablespoon cornstarch dissolved in 2 tablespoons water
2 egg whites

This soup is somewhat different in taste from the corn soup in Western cooking, and is, in fact, a rather extravagant dish.

Calories 95	Protein 6.3g	Fats 2.0g	Carbohydrates 12.1g

1. Purée chicken breast in a food processor or blender. Add water gradually and blend it thoroughly. Add rice wine and ginger juice and mix until very smooth.
2. Combine corn in a saucepan with chicken broth and salt and bring to a boil. Lower heat and add dissolved cornstarch and stir until soup thickens.

3. Beat egg whites until stiff but not dry, and slowly fold into chicken.
4. Add chicken and egg whites to corn. Mix it briefly with a whisk and bring to a second boil. When chicken and egg whites turn white, turn off heat. Be careful not to overboil, or egg whites will curdle.

Egg Drop Soup with Tomatoes

4 servings
Cooking time:
15 minutes
2 ripe tomatoes
½ onion
2 tablespoons vegetable oil
2 tablespoons sliced canned
  mushrooms
4 cups chicken broth
1½ teaspoons salt
Twist of black pepper
1 tablespoon ketchup
1 egg

A refreshingly light taste in a soup that's a cinch to make. The egg should not be allowed to solidify in one heavy mass but should be expanded like thin paper.

Calories 129	Protein 5.1g	Fats 8.5g	Carbohydrates 7.6g

1. Discard stems and seeds from tomatoes and cut into 8 wedges each.
2. Peel onion and slice halves into thin pieces.
3. Heat oil and stir-fry onion until soft. Add tomatoes and mushrooms and stir again. Add chicken broth.
4. When chicken broth begins

to bubble, lower heat and simmer about 5 minutes. Season with salt, pepper, and ketchup.
5. Beat egg slightly, and add to soup in a trickle, stirring soup simultaneously. When egg seems half cooked, turn off heat. Be careful not to overcook egg, or it will become tough and stringy.

Four Treasures Soup

4 servings
Cooking time:
20 minutes
4 ounces (100g) boneless
  chicken breast
Seasoning for chicken:
  1 teaspoon rice wine
  ½ teaspoon fresh ginger juice
  ½ teaspoon cornstarch

The symbolic "four treasures" are of course the four solid ingredients in the soup. In Chinese cooking, the names of the dishes are often allusive in this way.

Calories 125	Protein 13.4g	Fats 6.1g	Carbohydrates 2.4g

1. Slice chicken breast diagonally into bite-size pieces. Season with rice wine and ginger juice. Sprinkle with cornstarch and mix lightly.

2. Cook quail eggs until hard boiled, then remove shells.
3. Slice abalone diagonally into thin pieces.
4. Slice bamboo shoots into

thin pieces.

5. Peel cucumber and slice diagonally into thin rounds.

6. Bring chicken broth to a boil. Add chicken and bring to a second boil. Reduce heat and skim off as much foam as possible. Add abalone, bamboo shoots, and mushrooms and simmer 5 minutes. Season with rice wine and salt. Add quail eggs and cucumber last and turn off heat.

8 quail eggs
2 ounces (50g) canned abalone
2 ounces (50g) canned bamboo shoots
1 small pickling cucumber
4 cups chicken broth
8 whole canned mushrooms
1 tablespoon rice wine
1½ teaspoons salt

Chicken and Vegetable Soup

An easy-to-make soup that will keep you from having to rely on store-bought chicken broth. The ingredients as well as the actual making of the soup require no fuss.

Calories 203	Protein 20.6g	Fats 10.3g	Carbohydrates 3.7g

4 servings
Cooking time:
1 hour
15 minutes

1. Place chicken in a bowl and pour a pot of boiling water over. Drain and place chicken in a pot. Add spring onion, ginger, and water. Bring to a boil, lower heat, and skim off as much foam as possible. Simmer 1 hour.

2. Cut Chinese cabbage into large pieces. Slice bamboo shoots into thin pieces.

3. Add Chinese cabbage and bamboo shoots to chicken soup. Bring soup back to a boil, then reduce heat and simmer until Chinese cabbage is soft. Season with rice wine and salt.

1 pound (500g) chicken parts, cut into pieces
2-inch (5cm) piece of spring onion
2 slices of fresh ginger
6 cups water
1 pound(500g)Chinese cabbage
2 ounces (50g) canned bamboo shoots
2 teaspoons rice wine
1½ teaspoons salt

Beancurd and Mushroom Soup

This popular vegetarian soup is just the thing to help keep you fit and healthy.

Calories 80	Protein 9.8g	Fats 4.5g	Carbohydrates 6.9g

4 servings
Cooking time:
20 minutes

1. Cut beancurd into 1½-inch (4cm) cubes.

2. Soak dried mushrooms in warm water until soft, then remove stems. Cut each diagonally into 2 to 3 pieces.

3. Slice bamboo shoots into thin pieces.

4. Bring chicken broth to a boil in a soup pot. Add mushrooms and simmer 15 minutes.

5. Add bamboo shoots and beancurd to soup and season with rice wine and salt. Bring to a second boil before serving.

1 square beancurd (tofu)
8 dried mushrooms
2 ounces (50g) canned bamboo shoots
4 cups chicken broth
1 tablespoon rice wine
1½ teaspoons salt

Beef Hot Pot

Hot Pot is a famous Northern winter dish. Traditionally, mainly lamb or mutton was used but now beef as well as lamb is used. The most important fact is that the meat must be sliced paper thin. Hot Pot provides a friendly atmosphere as everyone cooks his or her own portion.

Arrange meat and vegetables on a large platter on the table. Set the ingredients for seasoning sauce on the table also. Using an electric hot plate, heat a large pot of water and add a few spring onions, ginger slices, and pickled vegetables. When water comes to a boil, guests dip meat slice into broth to briefly cook it, then into sauce before eating. Add vegetables gradually, saving noodles for the end.

In China, there is a special pot used for this dish which has a chimney in the center and which is placed over heated charcoal for cooking.

Ingredients (4 servings):

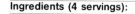

1½ pounds (750g) boneless beef or lamb, thinly sliced
½ pound (250g) Chinese cabbage, cut into bite-size pieces
½ pound (250g) Chinese green cabbage, cut into bite-size pieces
2 ounces (50g) bean thread noodles, soaked and cut

Condiments:

4 tablespoons finely julienned spring onions
2 tablespoons finely julienned fresh ginger
2 tablespoons coarsely chopped pickled vegetables
4 wedges lemon
4 sprigs of cilantro

Sauce (1 serving)*

1 tablespoon soy sauce
¼ teaspoon vinegar
¼ teaspoon hot bean paste, optional
1 teaspoon sesame paste
¼ teaspoon fermented beancurd
Pinch of salt

*Since everyone's taste differs, guests can prepare sauce to suit themselves or the host can prepare a number of different types of sauces from which they can choose.

Chinese Radish Consommé

Dried Mushroom Soup

Chinese Radish Consommé

4 servings
Cooking time:
3 hours
15 minutes
1 pound (500g) boneless
  beef shank
2-inch (5cm) piece of spring
  onion
1 slice of fresh ginger
8 cups water
10 ounces (300g) giant white
  radish
4 ounces (100g) carrot
1 tablespoon rice wine
1 tablespoon soy sauce
2 teaspoons salt
Twist of black pepper

The beef and radish in this soup need a long slow simmer. The result will be the release of the radish's sweetness and a taste that is out of this world.

Calories	213	Protein	27.8g	Fats	7.8g	Carbohydrates	5.0g

1. Cut beef into bite-size pieces. Place beef, spring onion, ginger, and water in a soup pot. When it comes to a boil, lower heat and skim off as much foam as possible. Simmer about 2 hours or until meat is tender.
2. Cut radish and carrot into large diagonal pieces.
3. Remove spring onion and ginger from soup and discard. Add carrot and radish. Bring to a second boil and lower flame. Simmer slowly another hour.
4. When radish and carrot pieces are tender, season soup with rice wine, soy sauce, salt, and pepper. Simmer another 10 minutes.

Dried Mushroom Soup

4 servings
Cooking time:
45 minutes,
plus cooking
time of broth
12 dried mushrooms
4 cups chicken broth using a
  whole chicken (see the
  Directions for Chicken Broth
  below)
1 teaspoon soy sauce
1 teaspoon salt
¼ teaspoon sugar
1-inch (2.5cm) piece of spring
  onion
2 slices of fresh ginger

A fragrantly elegant soup that is sure to please in China. Use thickly-lidded mushrooms of good quality, preferably in a home-made broth.

Calories	16	Protein	5.4g	Fats	0.9g	Carbohydrates	8.3g

1. Soak dried mushrooms in warm water until soft, then remove stems.
2. Prepare chicken broth and season with soy sauce, salt and sugar.
3. Place soup and mushrooms in a deep bowl and add spring onion and ginger. Cover the bowl.
4. Place the covered bowl in a steamer over high heat and steam about 30 minutes.
5. Skim off foam that floats to the surface of soup and remove spring onion and ginger before serving.

Chicken Broth Using a Whole Chicken

Chicken broth has a flavor that goes well with Chinese cooking and is often used in stir-fried recipes, dressings, and as a base for soups. It can be made and kept in the refrigerator to be used when needed. When preparing broth you may use either half a chicken or chunks of chicken, or to make the most delicious broth use a whole chicken. Since the chicken's delicious flavor goes into the broth, the best way to use the cooked chicken is to shred it for salads, sandwiches, or toppings.

Ingredients:
1 whole chicken	
½ spring onion	
1 slice of fresh ginger	
10 cups water	

Directions:

Wash a whole chicken and place it, with spring onion and ginger, in a soup pot. Cover with water. Bring the pot to a boil, uncovered, over high heat and just before it reaches a full boil, lower heat and skim off as much foam as possible. Cover the pot and simmer over very low heat 2 to 3 hours. When soup is reduced to two-thirds its original volume, strain it through a sieve.

DESSERTS

Since many dishes in Chinese cooking use oil, desserts have a big role to play as light, after-dinner taste fresheners. There is a large number to choose from, and their chief ingredients include wheat flour, rice or rice flour, fruit, various beans, and gelatin, with calories ranging widely from high to low. In the pages that follow I have tried to introduce some of the more traditional desserts as well as ones that, although using Chinese ingredients, have been given a modern twist.

Red Bean Sherbet
Almond Sherbet
Almond Gelatin with Lemon

Fruit Balls in Watermelon

Red Bean Sherbet

8 servings
Cooking time:
5 minutes
6 ounces (150g) sweet red bean paste
2 ounce (50g) muscovado
1 cup water
¾ cup milk

Sweet red bean paste is often used in China as a basis for a dessert. Canned paste is available and recommended.

Calories 74	Protein 1.5g	Fats 0.7g	Carbohydrates 15.5g

1. Combine sweet red bean paste, muscovado, and water into a pan. Put over medium heat and mix well with a small whisk till sweet red bean paste is completely dissolved. Skim off the mixture with a ladle occasionally while simmering. Remove.
2. Pour milk into another pan and put over medium heat. When it has begun to boil, turn off heat.
3. Pour the red been mixture into a bowl and add milk little by little mixing with a whisk.

4. Put the bowl in ice water and cool the mixture to room temperature occasionally stirring.
5. Freeze the mixture in ice cream maker or sorbetière, if available. If not, place the bowl in a freezer and when outer rim has begun to turn icy, remove the bowl from the freezer and whip the mixture until smooth. Repeat this procedure several times until it is smooth and yet still holds together.

Almond Sherbet

8 servings
Cooking time:
5 minutes
2 cups milk
4 ounces (100g) sugar
½ teaspoon almond extract

Iced desserts such as ice cream are high in calories but sherbet is lower. Sherbet is a type of dessert that goes well at the end of a Chinese meal. It can be prepared with various ingredients so there are endless variations.

Calories 78	Protein 1.5g	Fats 1.6g	Carbohydrates 14.7g

1. Combine milk and sugar into a pan, and put over medium heat till sugar is completely dissolved. Remove, add almond extract and mix well. Cool at room temperature.

2. Freeze the mixture in ice cream maker or sorbetière. If you do not have ice cream maker or sorbetière, place the mixture in a freezer and follow the directions for Red Bean Sherbet.

Almond Gelatin with Lemon

4 servings
Cooking time:
30 minutes
1 package unflavored gelatin
1 cup water
1 cup milk
4 ounces (100g) sugar
1 teaspoon almond extract
Syrup:
  2 cups water
  4 ounces (100g) sugar
4 slices of lemon

One of the most popular of the well-known Chinese desserts, perhaps because its sheer lightness on the palate is in such counterpoint to the oil-rich Chinese dishes. The flavor, of course, does not have to be lemon. Kiwi, orange, and even canned fruit give equally good results.

Calories 226	Protein 2.5g	Fats 1.6g	Carbohydrates 51.9g

1. Sprinkle gelatin over half of 1 cup water to soften.
2. Pour the remaining water into a pan, add milk and sugar. Put over low heat till sugar is

completely dissolved. Remove, add almond extract and mix well.
3. Pour into a bowl in which you will be serving gelatin, and chill it in the refrigerator.

4. Bring 2 cups of water to a boil and add sugar, stirring until sugar dissolves. This syrup needs to be chilled, so it may be made well in advance.

5. Cut gelatin diagonally into diamond shapes and pour cold syrup over. Garnish with lemon to serve (photos A, B).

A. Cut chilled gelatin diagonally into diamond shapes.

B. When syrup is poured, diamond shapes come out clearly and it is pleasing to the eye.

Fruit Balls in Watermelon

This beautifully decorative dessert is fancy enough for a party. In China, the usual thing is to make the carvings on the outer skin of the watermelon match the theme of the party in some way. Let preference and color govern your choice of fruit.

Calories 220	Protein 3.3g	Fats 0.2g	Carbohydrates 55.8g

**6 servings
Cooking time:
15 minutes**

1 medium watermelon
1 small honeydew melon
1 papaya
Syrup:
  4 ounces (100g) sugar
  2½ cups water

1. Bring 2½ cups of water to a boil and add sugar, stirring until sugar dissolves. Chill this syrup.
2. Prepare watermelon as illustrated on page 99. Use a small sharp knife and cut a large crescent shape out of both sides of watermelon about two-thirds of way up watermelon to form a handle. Carve a design in the skin of watermelon. Using a melon-baller, hollow out the inside of watermelon, and make as many balls as you can. Make some balls also out of honeydew and papaya.

3. Place assorted fruit balls into watermelon basket and pour syrup over fruits.
4. Chill fruits for several hours before serving.
Note: To stabilize watermelon so that it stands well, take a knife and cut a slice off the bottom, without cutting away meat. If you have difficulty making a handle, you may serve basket without a handle. You may also add fruit punch or juice instead of syrup.

Steamed Sponge Cakes

Fried Sweet Sesame Balls

Chinese Tapioca Pudding

Eight Treasures Rice Pudding

Steamed Sponge Cakes

6 servings
Cooking time:
40 minutes
4 eggs
6 ounces (150g) sugar
6 ounces (150g) all-purpose
flour
2 tablespoons coarsely
chopped walnuts
2 tablespoons coarsely
chopped Chinese dates

What makes this Chinese Sponge Cake so different is that it is steamed rather than baked in an oven. The walnuts and Chinese dates inside add to the difference, but it is the steaming that gives it that special texture and flavor.

Calories 274	Protein 6.7g	Fats 6.5g	Carbohydrates 46.9g

1. Whip eggs until frothy and add half of sugar and whip it again until fluffy. Add the remaining sugar and whip 10 minutes.
2. Sift flour and fold it into egg mixture.
3. Grease a 9-inch (22cm) square pan and fold in half the batter. Sprinkle with half of wal-nuts and dates and pour the rest of batter over them. Sprinkle the remaining walnuts and dates on top.
4. Stream 20 minutes over high heat.
5. Cut into small squares to serve.

Fried Sweet Sesame Balls

Makes about
20 balls
Cooking time:
30 minutes
½ cup sugar
1 egg
1 tablespoon vegetable oil
3 tablespoons water
1½ cups all-purpose flour
½ teaspoon baking powder
3 tablespoons white sesame
seeds
3 to 4 cups oil for deep-frying
1 teaspoon confectioners' sugar

These are not only simple to make, they're also fun. In Chinese they're called "Laughing Balls", because as they cook they open slightly like a smiling mouth. They're the kind of sweet that children especially will love.

Calories 78	Protein 1.2g	Fats 4.0g	Carbohydrates 8.9g

(1 ball)

1. Combine sugar, egg, oil, and water and mix well.
2. Sift flour and baking powder into the above mixture and mix well (photo A).
3. Knead dough and divide into small balls. Roll balls in sesame seeds until well coated (photo B). If seeds do not stick well to balls,
moisten with a little water and roll again.
4. Heat oil for deep-frying to 280°F (140°C) and deep-fry balls until golden brown. Remove from oil and drain well (photo C).
5. Place on a plate and sprinkle with confectioners' sugar to serve.

A. Combine sugar, egg, oil, and water. Sift flour and baking powder into the mixture and mix well.

B. Form dough into small balls and coat with sesame seeds.

C. Turn heat up just before balls are thoroughly done to make light and dry.

Chinese Tapioca Pudding

This warm dessert with sweet red bean paste in the center has enough flair about it to make it the kind of dish to serve when company comes. It can be made in individual dessert dishes or served from one large dish at the table.

| Calories 346 | Protein 7.2g | Fats 13.9g | Carbohydrates 47.0g |

**4 servings
Cooking time:
30 minutes**

1⅔ cups milk
3 tablespoons tapioca
1 tablespoon all-purpose flour
½ tablespoon cornstarch
7 tablespoons sugar
6 ounces (150g) sweet red bean paste
2 tablespoons butter
4 egg yolks
1 teaspoon confectioners' sugar

1. Preheat an oven to 350°F (180°C).
2. Heat 1 cup of milk with tapioca until tapioca softens.
3. Sift flour with cornstarch into another pan and gradually mix in sugar. Slowly add the remaining ⅔ cup of milk and mix well. Heat over medium flame, stirring constantly with a wooden spoon to prevent sticking.
4. Heat sweet red bean paste and butter, and mixing until well blended.
5. Combine the two mixtures by adding tapioca mixture into flour mixture. Heat and mix well. Remove the pan from flame and quickly whip egg yolks in. Return to medium flame for 1 to 2 minutes. Do not overheat, or egg yolks will separate and spoil pudding.
6. Pour ¼ of sweet bean mixture into each of 4 oven-proof custard cups and pour ¼ of custard mixture over sweet bean mixture.
7. Bake about 10 to 15 minutes or until surface is lightly browned.
8. Sprinkle with confectioners' sugar before serving.

Eight Treasures Rice Pudding

This is something akin to the Western decorative fruit cake, a veritable treasure-trove of goodies but in a pudding rather than in a cake. The "treasures", of course, are the glazed and colorful fruits.

| Calories 176 | Protein 2.5g | Fats 2.0g | Carbohydrates 36.5g |

**8 servings
Cooking time:
1 hour
30 minutes**

1 cup glutinous (sweet) rice
1 cup water
½ tablespoon lard or vegetable shortening
1 tablespoon sugar
6 ounces (150g) sweet red bean paste
2 whole candied cherries
4 whole candied apricots
3 candied Chinese dates
4 pitted prunes
1 green angelica
1 tablespoon orange peel
Syrup:
   3 tablespoons sugar
   ½ cup water
   1 tablespoon cornstarch dissolved in 2 tablespoons water

1. Wash glutinous rice well. Cover with water and let it soak 4 to 5 hours. Rinse rice and drain well.
2. Place rice in a bowl and add 1 cup of water. Steam rice 1 hour. When rice is cooked, add lard and sugar and mix well.
3. Heat sweet red bean paste over low flame, taking care not to burn and stirring until wateriness disappears.
4. Cut up dried fruits appropriately.
5. Brush a large oven-proof bowl with lard and arrange fruits in the bottom of the bowl as illustrated on page 103. Pour ¾ of rice into the bowl. Place sweet red bean paste in the center of rice, and cover with the remaining rice.
6. Cook in a steamer over high heat 15 minutes. Remove the bowl from the steamer and turn over onto a plate pudding side out with fruits side on top.
7. Combine sugar and water in a saucepan. Heat over low flame 5 minutes and add dissolved cornstarch. Stir quickly until syrup thickens.
8. Pour thickened syrup over pudding and cut into individual portions to serve.

Regional Variation of Chinese Cooking

China is a vast country with a long history and rich cultural heritage. As a result, Chinese cooking has a wide variety of styles, which are directly related to their geographical location.

Chinese culture developed along the major rivers. There was much activity along the river, where people found ways to make a living and cities grew from these people. Chinese cooking has developed from ancient times up to the present, paralleling the growth of Chinese civilization.

A map of China will clearly show the several important Chinese rivers. The Yellow River runs through Northern China and the Yangtze River divides Central China. The Pearl River runs through the South. Chinese cooking can therefore be roughly divided into the regions of north, south, east and west, which is basically how the great rivers of China divide the country. The cooking of these regions is directly related to the geography, climate, and growing conditions.

Southern: Cantonese cooking

Canton and Hong Kong lie in the heart of the southern Pearl River region. This region is blessed with a warm climate and a great variety of products. Being close to the ocean, there is also an abundance of fresh seafood. There is an old Chinese saying which says that the best scenery in China is in Hanchow, the prettiest girls in Soochow and the best food to be found in Canton. The great interest in food in the South is reflected in the captivating flavors of southern style cooking. Cantonese food has come to be the most widely known of all Chinese cooking styles. It is renowned for the freshness and the variety of the ingredients. Perhaps this is why Cantonese food is sometimes the least complicated of the various Chinese regional foods, delicately seasoned and retaining the vital freshness of the ingredients. Because of its location as a seaport and increased relations with the Western world, Cantonese cooking has also been influenced by such foreign foods as milk, beef (which was traditionally not eaten as oxen were important as working farm animals), butter, and tomato ketchup, which has now become a part of Cantonese cooking. In fact, the word "ketchup" is a direct translation in Chinese for "tomato (ke) sauce (chup)".

Northern or "Peking" food

The most representative style of cooking in the northern Yellow River basin is Peking (Beijing) and Shantung cooking. Beijing has long been the capital of China as well as its political, economic and cultural center. Accordingly, Beijing cooking also developed to a high degree, including the special style of cooking called "Imperial Cooking" which was served only to the Emperor. "Peking Duck" is a dish known all over the world and is representative of Imperial Cooking. The Northern region produces wheat as a main crop and therefore gave rise to many flour-based dishes, such as dumplings, buns, and a variety of noodles. Northern people as a result often eat much more flour-based food than rice. North of the Yellow River, there are more stir-fried or fried foods, while south of the river, soups are a more characteristic part of the cuisine.

Eastern: Shanghai cooking

Shanghai is located in the easternmost part of China at the mouth of the Yangtze River. The cuisine of this great city is representative of this region. Due to its location bordering both the sea and the river, fish and shellfish are an integral part of the cuisine. Rice is eaten more than the flour-based foods of the North. Some of the seafood comes from fresh waters, and shrimp is an important part of Shanghai style food. One special sauce from this area is a slightly thick sauce made from soy sauce, and sweetened with a little sugar. There are also quite a number of stewed dishes.

Western: Szechuan cooking

The upper region of the Yangtze River has two major cities: Chendu and Chongqing (Chunking). Szechuan cooking is reflected in the cooking of these two cities. This well watered region abounds in a variety of vegetables and small river fishes. One regional specialty is rock salt, which is widely used in their cuisine. Another characteristic is the wide use of spring onions and garlic, as well as a variety of preserved or pickled vegetables. Because of the severe winters in the mountains of Szechuan, chili peppers and hot red beanpaste are used as spices in many dishes. In the minds of many people, as a result, Szechuan has become synonymous with "hot and spicy".

How to Use Wok and Steamer

The Chinese wok

"Wok" is simply the Cantonese pronunciation of the Chinese word for "pan". In Mandarin the same word would be "guo".

The shape of the wok is round and deeper than the Western frying pan, especially in the center. This allows for even distribution of heat so that foods may be cooked quickly and evenly. Due to its versatility, it can be used for stir-frying, deep-frying, stewing and steaming.

Woks come with either one handle, as in a Western frying pan, or with two handles. A one-handled wok is very useful for stir-frying, as you can have a firm grip on the wok with one hand while stirring with the other. A wok with two handles is more useful for steaming and stewing, but can easily be used for stirring as well.

The traditional wok is made of iron and its surface improves with use and correct care. When breaking in a new wok, it is helpful to fill it with water and scrub it with a scouring pad to remove the protective coating of oil. Dry it thoroughly and heat the empty wok over high heat, until it is very hot. Add a generous amount of oil, anywhere from a half to a full cup depending on the size, and turn the wok several times to make sure the oil coats the whole surface. Discard this oil and your wok is ready to use.

When you are cooking with a wok, always remember to heat the wok over high heat before adding the oil and make sure the cooking surface is well coated with the oil before adding the ingredients.

When you have finished cooking with the wok, add some hot water to the wok with the flame still on and clean it with a mildly abrasive scouring pad until it is clean. Pour out the water and wipe it with a cloth and finish drying it over the flame until it is completely dry.

The Chinese steamer

The Chinese steamer is made of wood and bamboo and has remained unchanged over the years. We recommend using a bamboo steamer, but if it is unavailable, a metal one may be substituted. The diameter of the bamboo steamer should be slightly smaller than the wok so that it rests firmly in the wok.

Fill the bottom of the wok with water and first wet the bottom of the wood or bamboo so that it will not burn, before placing it on the wok. Place the bamboo steamer over the water and bring it to a boil. Place the food on the racks of the steamer and cover it tightly so no steam escapes. Fish or meat may be steamed on plates. You may use only one rack, or place several on top of each other. Dumplings and buns may be steamed on a tea towel or cheesecloth.

Cutting Techniques

Mastering Chinese cooking involves practicing different cutting methods. Practice will make perfect, and should be done in a relaxed manner. There is an old Chinese saying which says that the flavor of a dish reflects the mood of the cook and his cutting ability. If time is of the essence, you may do certain kinds of cutting in the food processor.

The most important principle in cutting is to remember that the main ingredients of a dish should be cut in approximately the same size as the secondary ingredients. When you cook them, you must take into consideration the speed at which different foods cook and add them in such a sequence that none of the ingredients will be either overcooked or undercooked.

Thin Slicing

To cut into thin slices, hold knife at a perpendicular angle to the cutting board.
Photo A Cut carrot into 2-inch (5cm) lengths, and slice them vertically into thin slices.
Photo B Cut cucumber into half and slice them diagonally into thin pieces.
Photo C Cut bamboo shoot in half and slice them vertically into thin pieces with cut section downward. If bamboo shoot is large, cut it into half lengthwise before cutting into half horizontally.

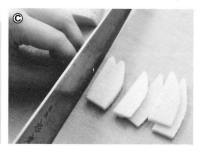

Slicing Diagonally

Slicing diagonally is recommended for any meat, fish, or vegetables when the slices need to be thin.

Place the ingredient to be sliced on the cutting board and hold it firmly with your left hand. Hold the knife in your right hand and slice down, slanting the blade at a diagonal angle.
Photo D After soaking dried mushroom and removing the stem, slice them diagonally into 2 to 3 pieces.
Photo E Remove any tendon and skin from chicken and slice diagonally.

Cutting into Strips or Julienne

Cutting into thin strips in French cooking is called a "julienne". Because of the widespread use of this word, we have chosen to use this term, which best describes the Chinese style of cutting into thin strips. For a fine julienne, slice the ingredients thinly and slowly slide them toward the blade and slice them into thin strips. This method is especially important in some meat dishes when it is necessary to cut against the grain of the meat. This allows the strips to cook easily.
Photo F Peel ginger and slice into a fine julienne.
Photo G Slice meat thinly and again into a fine julienne.
Photo H Slice green bell pepper into half and remove the stem and seeds. Cut into julienne.

Chopping

Cut the ingredients into strips and follow this by cutting the strips into fine pieces.

Photo I Finely chopped ginger is used to season many stir-fried dishes.

Photo J To chop the spring onions coarsely, cut them first into quarters and then chop them into fine pieces.

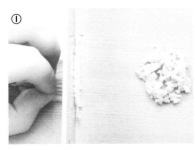

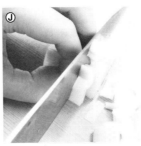

Squared Strips

Photo K Cut carrot into 2-inch (5cm) long pieces and then into ½-inch (1cm) squared sticks.

Dicing

Vegetables, meats, and a variety of other ingredients are often diced into ½-inch (1cm) cubes.

Photo L Cut carrot into squared strips and then dice them into ½-inch (1cm) cubes.

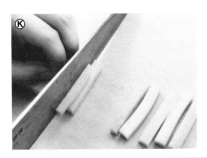

Cutting into Odd Shapes

Both round and long ingredients are often sliced diagonally but alternating the direction of the knife so that you get triangular-shaped pieces. This can be done with whole carrots and cucumbers, while larger vegetables such as giant white radish should be cut into half first.

Photo M Peel carrot and slice diagonally, turning round the carrot.

Technical Advice for Chinese Cooking

Seasoning before Cooking

In cooking Chinese food, most stir-frying recipes call for the main ingredients of meat, fish or poultry to be lightly seasoned before cooking. Light seasoning releases the flavors of meats, guards against toughening, and preserves the shape of the meat. Light seasoning also cuts the strong flavors of meat, fish and poultry. Although the ingredients and steps of different recipes vary, the basic rules of seasoning remain the same. Add the seasoning and mix the ingredients well. Marinate all this briefly and sprinkle lightly with cornstarch (photo A). Cornstarch also gives the ingredients a soft texture.

The Use of Dissolved Cornstarch and Thickened Sauces

Cornstarch which has been mixed with water until it is smooth is often added just before the heat is turned off to thicken the juices to make the sauce. The amount of cornstarch used in different recipes varies, but the basic rule is to dissolve one part of cornstarch in two parts of water (photo B). When the ingredients in the wok are cooked to just the right degree, stir the dissolved cornstarch with a spoon and pour it into the wok just before turning off the flame. Stir the combined ingredients in the wok quickly until the sauce thickens. Turn off the heat and serve immediately.

There are two kinds of thickened sauces which are poured over dishes. One is made for stir-fried or deep-fried dishes such as Sweet and Sour Pork (page 46). The other kind of thickened sauce is for steamed or stewed dishes such as Steamed Whitefish with Ham and Mushrooms (page 30). Thickened sauces are made by thickening the juices or soup of dishes with cornstarch.

●Points to Remember about Dishes with Thickened Sauces
1. Dishes which have a thickened sauce to pour over should be lightly seasoned so that both flavors of the sauce and the main dish blend.
2. The timing of combining the main dish and the sauce is important. Always make the main dish before the sauce.
3. Always mix the cornstarch and water until it is smooth. Otherwise you will have lumps, unattractive as well as unappetizing. Stop cooking as soon as the sauce thickens, or it will bocome dry.

Stir-Frying

Stir-frying is a style of cooking which retains the color and the fresh flavor of vegetables by cooking them in a small amount of oil quickly over a high heat. The combination of seasoning and stir-frying meats, fish and poultry retains the natural juices and flavors of the ingredients.

All the ingredients in any given recipe should be cut into similar sizes and shapes. They should be cooked over high and even heat until they are just cooked and pleasing to the eye. Always judge by tasting as you go along and correct the seasoning.

In many traditional Chinese recipes, the main ingredients of meat, fish or poultry are first quickly stir-fried in hot oil until the color changes. The oil used to do this is not as hot as for deep-frying and the purpose of this process is to tenderize the ingredients as well as to prevent them from sticking together. In this book, this process, as well as large amounts of oil, has been carefully reduced to give the same results, but with less calories and a more healthful effect.

●Points to Remember in Stir-Frying
1. Make sure your ingredients are completely dry as any excess moisture when placed into oil will cause dangerous splattering.
2. Remember to turn the wok and make sure the surface of the wok is coated with oil so that foods will not stick and burn.
3. Use high heat and turn the ingredients quickly from the bottom of the wok upwards with the spatula.
4. Remember to consider the order of the ingre-

dients which are to be cooked. Spring onions, ginger, garlic or other herbs should always be stir-fried first. In stir-frying recipes, vegetables and meats are cooked separately and then combined. In the case of Beef with Green Bell Peppers (page 35), stir-fry green bell peppers and remove. Then stir-fry beef, and season. Finally return green bell peppers. (photo C).

Deep-Frying

Deep-frying is a style of cooking which retains the flavors of ingredients by immersing them in a wok of oil over heat till they become crisp and cooked all through.

●Points to Remember in Deep-Frying
1. Ingredients should be cut in uniform size in the same cutting manner. Uneven size will cause uneven cooking.
2. Give the ingredients light seasoning before cooking. This is characteristic of Chinese fried dishes.
3. Prepare plenty of frying oil, enough for the ingredients to be completely immersed. The temperature of a large amount of oil is more stable.
4. Put a moderate amount of ingredients into the oil. Putting too much at once into the oil will lower the temperature, and it will take some time for the oil to return to the right temperature. That will affect the finish.
5. The temperature of oil should be kept between 320°F and 380°F (between 160°C and 190°C).
6. The trick is to finally turn up the heat to between 360°F and 380°F (between 180°C and 190°C). Scoop all the ingredients at once (photo D). It will prevent uneven cooking and the finish will be pleasing to the eye.

Stewing

In Chinese cooking, raw ingredients are some-times stewed, but usually ingredients are stir-fried, deep-fried or steamed before being stewed. Stewed foods are usually sautéed, seasoned, and then simmered in water or soup. In the case of Stewed Acorn Squash (page 55), stir-fry squash, season, and add water, then stew slowly until squash is tender (photo E).

●Points to Remember in Stewing
1. Bring the soup or broth to a boil over high heat. Just before the soup reaches a full boil, skim off foam. Reduce the heat and simmer.
2. When stewing meat that has good flavor, you may use water instead of broth. In the case of vegetables or dried ingredients which have less flavor, it is best to use a broth with good flavor.
3. Remember to add the ingredients in the order of the speed at which they cook, those that cook the slowest should be added first.
4. Remember to season stews or soups lightly to begin with, keeping in mind that the liquid will reduce, which will make the flavors stronger.

Steaming

"Steaming" is effective in retaining the ingredients' flavors and nutrition, because it heats the ingredients indirectly with steam.

●Points to Remember in Steaming
1. Make sure the ingredients are dry and season them evenly.
2. Place the steamer cover on the wok with water in it. When the water comes to a full boil, place the steamer racks in the wok and cover it tightly, to make sure no steam escapes (photo F).
3. Always steam at very high heat, unless the dish requires prolonged steaming, in which case, you may steam at moderate heat.
4. Never remove the cover while you are steaming, keeping the heat even.
5. It is best to use ovenproof or ceramic dishes to steam in since they absorb heat well.
6. Remember to check the water level, especially in prolonged steaming.

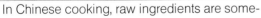

Suggested Menus for Health and Fitness

Foods and Health

Leading a healthful life involves more than just eating the proper foods. As we all know, plenty of sleep and moderate exercise also play important roles. Even so, food does seem to be a factor of primary importance.

Some people seem convinced that all it takes for health and fitness is to eat, say, lots of rice or lots of beancurd (tofu). That, however, is a mistaken way of thinking, for no single food has yet been found that alone is capable of sustaining life. Even the egg—the so-called "perfect food"—cannot do it, and anyone who tries to live solely on eggs does so at the risk of becoming totally debilitated.

Meals for health and fitness should be based on a nutritional balance and the right caloric intake. To achieve a nutritional balance a combination of many foods, not just one single item, should be eaten. The simplest way to do this is to combine foods from each of the four major food groups: (1) protein from fish and shellfish; (2) carbohydrates from grains, cereals, tubers, fats and oils; (3) vitamins from fruits and vegetables; (4) nutritional supplements from eggs and dairy products.

In regard to calories, needs differ according to a person's age, sex, physical activity level and other individual differences, so that probably the safest generalization one can make is to suggest that a person stop short of eating to the point of fullness, making 70 to 80 percent of fullness the goal.

An ideal way to consider nutritional balance and caloric intake is in terms of daily consumption as opposed to consumption per meal, which is too short, or consumption per week, which is too long. To expect everything to go just as planned would hardly be realistic, but if you can at least get close to your daily consumption goal and then establish that as a dietary habit, you will have a good start on your way to health and fitness.

Menu Planning

In China, the general order of dishes at a banquet is appetizers first, followed by various other dishes, then soup and dessert. Unlike the order in western meals, soup is served toward the end and signals the conclusion of the meal.

In the home, however, banquet-type menus are not closely followed. You can freely make up your own, even omitting the appetizers, soup and dessert to make just a two-course meal plus tea. The important thing is to vary the dishes and cooking methods, serve hot foods hot, cold foods cold, and make combinations on the basis of the time and effort required to prepare them.

Example Menus for Health and Fitness

The four Lunch Menus and six Dinner Menus introduced on the following pages are made up from recipes that appear in various sections of this book. The Lunch Menus are designed as light meals, and the Dinner Menus as the most substantial meals of the day. You should, however, feel free to switch them around if you prefer your biggest meal in the middle of the day and a light one at the end.

Each menu incorporates the nutritional balance needed for health and fitness in addition to providing the caloric value per person. Allowances must of course be made for individual differences, but I have used the generally accepted figure of 1600 to 1800 calories daily as the amount needed to maintain good health, parcelling this out at anywhere from 300 to 700 calories per meal.

Dinner Menu (6) has been made as a party menu for a large number of people, but in all the other menus a standard of four has been used. Should you want to reduce the number to two, you can generally do so by halving the ingredients called for in the recipes.

Lunch Menu (1)

	Calories	Page

Colorful and light-tasting fried rice paired up with a quickly-made soup. Big eaters may bemoan the quantity, but the calories and nutritional balance provide an ample light lunch. To lower the calories even more you can halve the soup measurements on page 92, leaving the fried rice as it is. For the fried rice you will first need to cook up a batch of plain rice. Directions for this are on page 76. You will find it handy if you make a large amount ahead of time and freeze it in portions called for in the recipe.

	Calories	Page
Fried Rice with Crabmeat and Lettuce	257	74
Egg-Drop Soup with Tomatoes	129	90
Total	386	

Lunch Menu (2)

A light lunch even lower in calories than Menu (1). To obtain a nutritional balance I have made meat the filling for one bun and spinach for the other, but if calories are of concern they can be lowered by putting spinach in both. For a beverage I have suggested tea, either Chinese Oolong or western tea, although the calories will rise for the latter if you use sugar. Each teaspoon has approximately 10 calories. You can substitute soup for tea, with a slight rise in calories. Select from those in the Soup Section or use an instant one.

	Calories	Page
Chinese Steamed Buns		
(Meat bun 1)	101	82
(Spinach bun 1)	88	82
Tea (or Soup)		
Total	189	

Lunch Menu (3)

A menu suitable for a family Sunday lunch. The making of the meat pies can be an enjoyable hands on affair for the whole family. Three each for the adults should keep you within the requirements of health and fitness, but growing and hungry children can easily handle four. A good partner for this dish is a vegetable salad. To keep the fixing easy I have suggested a simple one of french dressing over vegetables, although you are certainly welcome to make a light salad of your own choosing if you prefer.

	Calories	Page
Chinese Pan-Fried Meat Pie (3)	201	79
Vegetable Salad	100	
Total	301	

Lunch Menu (4)

A lunch more substantial in volume than the three listed above. Grains are in the majority so it may seem to be nothing but carbohydrates, but as moderate amounts of meat and vegetables are used the overall nutritional balance is by no means bad. The dumplings can be decreased for those who feel there are too many. By making more than needed you can freeze the excess, as dumplings can also be steamed or fried in oil. Since the menu needs to be complemented by something liquid, tea or soup is suggested as in Menu (2).

	Calories	Page
Poached Chinese Dumplings (6)	192	78
Fried Rice with Spinach	231	74
Tea (or Soup)		
Total	423	

Dinner Menu (1)

A menu for health and fitness featuring seafood as the main dish. Both appetizers and salad have been omitted, which is nothing for concern in a dinner menu for home-style Chinese cooking. The menu brings together items that have light and simple flavors, with the protein in the shrimp and beancurd complementing the carbohydrates in the vegetables and grains for a nutritionally sound meal. The seasonings provide additional variety.

Should you want to decrease the calories you can reduce the amount of rice. Each six-ounce serving of plain rice per person is 200 calories.

	Calories	Page
Shrimp with Vegetables	144	22
Beancurd with Oyster Sauce	130	67
Chicken and Corn Soup	95	90
Plain Rice (6 ounces/150 g)	200	76
Total	569	

Dinner Menu (2)

A family-style dinner menu using seafood as the main dish, salad as an appetizer, and soup. You will need to increase the variety of appetizers if an appreciable amount of alcohol is served, but otherwise you can stay with the quantity given in the recipe.

Since a meal centering on seafood can easily degenerate into blandness, it is necessary to use a variety of seasonings. Oyster sauce in particular not only makes food taste good but provides an easy way to give variety to a meal at the planning stage.

For the calorie-conscious, the plain rice can be reduced as in Dinner Menu (1) or bread can be substituted for the rice.

	Calories	Page
Crabmeat and Chicken Salad	104	14
Scallops with Oyster Sauce	154	22
Egg-Drop Soup with Tomatoes	129	90
Plain Rice (6 ounces/150 g)	200	76
Total	587	

Dinner Menu (3)

A dinner menu that takes beef as its main course. Meats—not only beef—tend to increase the caloric content of a meal. However, depending on the particular cut, cooking method and accompanying foods, it is really not so difficult to control the calories and achieve a nutritional balance. For health and fitness, round or other similar cuts with little fat make a wise choice, and simmering or steaming is better than frying. For nutritional balance, meat dishes should also incorporate plenty of vegetables. In this menu I have included tomatoes, eggplants, and Chinese cabbage.

Since meat dishes are important in adding variety to meals, you should try out those that go with health and fitness.

	Calories	Page
Tomato Beef	209	34
Eggplants with Soy Dressing	45	50
Chicken and Vegetable Soup	203	91
Plain Rice (6 ounces/150 g)	200	76
Total	657	

Dinner Menu (4)

	Calories	Page
Curried Beef with Onions	380	38
String Beans and Tomatoes	85	55
Beancurd and Mushroom Soup	80	91
Plain Rice (3 ounces/80 g)	100	76
Total	645	

Another dinner plan featuring a main course of simmered beef but with more meat-calories than in Menu (3). To keep to the needs for health and fitness, the calories and nutritional balance will have to be smoothed out by adjustments in the other dishes. This can often be easily achieved by using fresh vegetables, but such processed vegetable foods as beancurd and dried mushrooms work equally well. Both contain nutritional elements not found in meat, and being low in calories will not add much to the overall caloric intake. They also add variety to a meal.

The amount of plain rice has been cut in half to keep the calories low, but the overall volume of the meal is sufficient.

Dinner Menu (5)

	Calories	Page
Salmon and Beancurd Salad	136	14
Chicken with Oyster Sauce	338	42
Sautéed Tomatoes	80	51
Plain Rice (3 ounces/80 g)	100	76
Total	654	

An example of a menu featuring a main course of chicken. The section of chicken highest in calories is the fatty skin. There is otherwise no appreciable difference in the calories in the thighs or the breasts. For health and fitness it is suggested that you remove the skin when cooking with chicken.

Chicken itself has a rather simple flavor which can easily be altered by seasoning or the way it is cooked. In the menu at hand, the oyster sauce imparts a flavorful richness nicely balanced by the lightness of the other two dishes for an overall variety in tastes.

As in Menu (4), the amount of plain rice has been halved.

Dinner Menu (6)

	Calories	Page
Assorted Vegetable Salad	55	15
Chilled Beancurd Salad	73	66
Chicken with Garden Vegetables	115	42
Deep-Fried Mushrooms	67	11
Fish Toast with Ham	116	27
Chinese Radish Consommé	142	95
Fried Sweet Sesame Balls (2)	156	102
Total	724	

An example of a party menu for six to eight people. Since Menus (1)–(5) were designed for two to four people they do not provide enough food to make a party a success. When large numbers are involved, prime consideration has to be given to having enough food.

Menu-planning for large numbers demands more than just planning a varied menu. Other factors to be considered are cooking time, order of preparation, tableware, how much to spend and where to obtain the needed materials.

In the menu here I have assembled items that take little time to make, can be cooked together or ahead of time, and which contribute to health and fitness.

Glossary of Major Ingredients

This section briefly outlines the ingredients used in the recipes in this book. These ingredients are indispensable for Chinese cooking. (Alphabetically arranged)

BAMBOO SHOOT

Bamboo shoots are gathered in the springtime from the new shoots of bamboo trees. The shoot is peeled and boiled 2 or 3 hours to soften it. Canned bamboo shoots are already cooked and usually already sliced. If you are able to purchase whole shoots, slice them in half lengthwise and cut into thin slices or julienne them (photo A, B).

BEAN THREAD NOODLES

Bean thread noodles or Chinese vermicelli, as they are sometimes called, are made from pea-starch. These noodles have a firm texture, and boiling does not affect their firmness. They are widely used in stir-fried dishes, stews, cold dishes and soups.
Preparation: Soak them in a generous amount of warm water until they are soft. Wring out any excess water. If they are very long, they may be cut in half with scissors after you soak them (photo C).

BLACK BEAN PASTE

Black bean paste, or Hoisin sauce, is made from flour and malted rice. It has a dark brown color and is an essential sauce for Peking duck and Mandarin pancakes, but it is also used in other dishes.

CHINESE CABBAGE

Chinese cabbage is also sold as Bok Chay, its name in Cantonese. It has softer fibers and a higher water content than head cabbage. It is a staple food in China and used in stir-fried dishes, soups, and salads. When it is unavailable, you may substitute head cabbage (photo D).

CHINESE GREEN CABBAGE

Chinese green cabbage (qing geng cai) with deep green leaves and a thick white stalk is often used in soups as well as stir-fried dishes. This vegetable may be difficult to find in the West, in which case, you may substitute Chinese cabbage (photo E).

CHINESE NOODLES

Chinese noodles are made by adding jian shui, or a saturated solution of potassium carbonate, to dough and kneading it. They are sold as raw, steamed and dried noodles. Raw and dried noodles are used after being boiled leaving some of their firmness. They are used for soup noodles and chow mein. Shown in the photograph (from top clockwise) are steamed, raw and dried noodles (photo F).

CILANTRO

Cilantro is the Spanish name of Coriander. As it is widely used in Mexican food, it is now generally sold under this Spanish name. It is also known as Chinese parsley, and is a fragrant herb. It gives a distinctive flavor to foods and is often used as a garnish (photo G).

DRIED MUSHROOM

Dried mushrooms have a more fragrant flavor than fresh mushrooms and are an indispensable part of Chinese Cooking. They contain many vitamins and yet no calorie. There are many different grades of dried mushrooms. The highest grade have thick and only partially opened caps, along with star-like lines on their caps.
Preparation: Wash dried mush-

Ⓐ

Ⓑ

Ⓒ

Ⓓ

Ⓔ

Ⓕ

Ⓖ

rooms lightly, place them in a bowl and cover them with cold or lukewarm water. Soak them for 15 to 60 minutes. Cut off the hard tips of the stems. The water that they were soaked in is used as soup with fragrance (photo H).

DRIED RED PEPPER

Dried red peppers have a bright red color and are very hot. They are indispensable ingredients in certain dishes as well as pickles. They are also known for enhancing the appetite and as an aid in preservation. The stems and seeds should be removed (photo I).

DRIED SCALLOP

Dried scallops are an extremely high-grade ingredient used in soups and specialty dishes. They have a rich golden color and their original rounded shape is preserved through drying.

Preparation: Place the dried scallops in a bowl and cover them with boiling water. Soak them for 6 to 8 hours, or if you are using them for soup you may soak them even longer. Use them whole, or shred them into pieces by hand. The water that they were soaked in may be added to soups for added flavor (photo J).

FERMENTED BEANCURD

Fermented beancurd (tofu) is used for sauces or as a condiment to accompany Beef Hot Pot (page 94). It is made from salted beancurd which is drained and fermented.

GARLIC

Garlic is widely used in Chinese cooking. It is known for reducing any bitterness or strong smells of certain ingredients and has an aromatic flavor when cooked. Garlic is also believed to fight bacteria and to relieve fatigue (photo K).

GINGER

Ginger is a pungent root, one of the most used flavors in Chinese food. It reduces the strong taste and odors of fish, meat, and fowl. It is very often used in conjunction with spring onions in stir-frying. All the recipes in this book call for fresh ginger which should be peeled and sliced thinly. Soups and slowly cooked stews usually use ginger slices. Stir-fried dishes are either finely chopped or julienned ginger. When recipes call for ginger juice, use a fine grater to grate the ginger or chop it very finely and squeeze the juice out, discarding the pulp (photo L).

HOT BEAN PASTE

Hot bean paste (dou ban jiang) is made from fermented soy beans, and is flavored with spices and chili peppers. It has a thick consistency and is of a reddish color. It is used in sauces as well as stir-fried dishes, and also as a condiment. It adds a special taste to dishes and is widely used in Szechuan cuisine.

JELLYFISH

Jellyfish has a crunchy texture and is served as an appetizer. Since jellyfish is salted and preserved in sheets or in strips, it must be soaked.

Preparation: Soak the sheets of jellyfish in salted water overnight, making sure to clean both surfaces. Soak for another day in clear water. Rinse them and drain them well. Cut them into strips and cover them with hot water until they curl. Soak them again overnight and drain them. Rinse them well before you use them (photo M).

Ⓗ   Ⓙ   Ⓛ

Ⓘ   Ⓚ   Ⓜ

OYSTER SAUCE

Oyster sauce is made from fermented oysters, and has a sweet and salty flavor. The consistency is thick and the color is similar to that of Worcestershire sauce. Oyster sauce combined with a little soy sauce and salt enhances the flavor, and is widely used and well known in Cantonese cooking.

SESAME OIL

Sesame oil is a particularly fragrant oil and only a small amount is used. It greatly enhances the flavor of stir-fried dishes and dressings. Care should be taken not to use too much, as the flavor will overpower the flavor of the other ingredients (photo N).

SESAME SEEDS

There are two kinds, white and black sesame. Sesame seeds are rich in protein and used for pastries, dressings, some deep-fried dishes and also often used as a garnish. The seeds are used whole or lightly toasted and ground. When used freshly ground in dressed dishes and sesame dipping sauces, their distinctive flavor and aroma can be fully appreciated. Sesame paste made from whole sesame seeds is very fragrant. It lends a distinctive flavor to sauces, salad dressings, and many noodle dishes (photo O).

SPRING ONION

Spring onions, or long green onions, are widely used in Chinese cooking, particularly in conjunction with ginger, which lends a special flavor and aroma to the dishes. Spring onions are usually cut into thin slices or chopped. Sometimes they are cut into long diagonal pieces. They are also often used as a garnish (photo P).

STAR ANISE

Star anise comes from dried berries and is shaped like an eight-pointed star. It is an important ingredient in Five-Spice Powder which includes star anise, fennel, cloves, Japanese Pepper and cinnamon. It has a special flavor and adds a fragrant touch to meats, fish and fowl (photo Q).

SWEET RED BEAN PASTE

Sweet red bean paste is made by boiling red bean paste till it is soft, straining it, adding sugar to it and boiling again till it is pasty. It is available in cans and used for sweets.

WOOD-EAR MUSHROOM

The wood-ear mushroom is a kind of ear-shaped bracket fungus found growing on the bark of mulberry and oak tree trunks. It is preserved by drying and has little flavor, but a wonderfully smooth texture and shiny black color. In addition to black wood-ear mushrooms, there is also a white variety, used mainly for desserts.

Preparation: Soak dried wood-ear mushrooms in a generous amount of hot water until they expand to about five times their original size. Pick them over to remove any hard sections and rinse off any surface dirt (photo R).

ZHA CAI

Zha cai is a specialty product of Szechuan which is famous for pickled vegetables. Zha cai is made from the root of the mustard plant and has a slight hot flavor. It is usually sold in cans or jars and is used in soups, stir-fried dishes, and stews. Wash the chili peppers off before you use it unless you want the hot taste (photo S).

Ⓝ

Ⓞ WEL·PAC SHIRO GOMA WHITE SESAME SEEDS 白胡麻   WEL·PAC KURO GOMA BLACK SESAME SEEDS 黒胡麻

Ⓟ

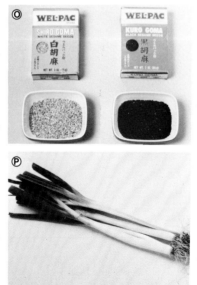

Ⓠ

Ⓡ

Ⓢ

Index

Tomato	90·92
Sautéed Tomato	51·53
String Beans and Tomatoes	55·57
Tomato Beef	34·36

Assorted Vegetables

Assorted Vegetable Salad	15·17
Chicken with Garden Vegetables	42·44
Szechuan Pickled Vegetables	50·52

Egg

Baked Crabmeat Omelet	63·65
Egg Drop Soup with Tomatoes	90·92
Egg Foo Yong	62·64
Mu Shu Pork	62·64
Shrimp and Scrambled Egg	86·88
Steamed Custard with Clams	63·65

Beancurd

| Beancurd and Fish Soup | 70·69 |

Beancurd and Meatball Soup	71·72
Beancurd and Mushroom Soup	91·93
Beancurd with Crabmeat	67·68
Beancurd with Ground Pork	70·72
Beancurd with Oyster Sauce	67·69
Chilled Beancurd Salad	66·68
Salmon and Beancurd Salad	14·16
Spicy Beancurd Salad	66·68

Rice

Beef and Vegetable Rice	75·77
Curried Lamb and Rice	75·77
Fried Rice with Crabmeat and Lettuce	74·76
Fried Rice with Spinach	74·76

Pasta

| Chinese Pan-Fried Meat Pie | 79·81 |

Chinese Steamed Buns	82·84
Fried Noodles with Beef	83·85
Fried Noodles with Vegetables	83·85
Mandarin Pancakes	86·88
Poached Chinese Dumplings	78·80
Siu Mai	82·84
Vermicelli Salad	14·16

Desserts

Almond Gelatin with Lemon	98·100
Almond Sherbet	98·100
Chinese Tapioca Pudding	103·105
Eight Treasures Rice Pudding	103·105
Fried Sweet Sesame Balls	102·104
Fruit Balls in Watermelon	99·101
Red Bean Sherbet	98·100
Steamed Sponge Cakes	102·104